OUR SCHOOLS IN WAR TIME—AND AFTER

ARTHUR D. DEAN, Sc.D.

PROFESSOR OF VOCATIONAL EDUCATION, TEACHERS COLLEGE
COLUMBIA UNIVERSITY, AND SUPERVISING OFFICER
BUREAU OF VOCATIONAL TRAINING, NEW YORK
STATE MILITARY TRAINING COMMISSION

GINN AND COMPANY
BOSTON · NEW YORK · CHICAGO · LONDON
ATLANTA · DALLAS · COLUMBUS · SAN FRANCISCO

The Athenæum Press

GINN AND COMPANY · PRO-
PRIETORS · BOSTON · U.S.A.

FOREWORD

It is not an army that we must shape and train for war; it is a nation. . . . The whole nation must be a team in which each man shall play the part for which he is best fitted. . . . Each man shall be classified for service in the place to which it shall best serve the general good to call him. . . . The significance of this cannot be overstated. It is a new thing in our history and a landmark in our progress. It is a new manner of accepting and vitalizing our duty to give ourselves with thoughtful devotion to the common purpose of us all.— WOODROW WILSON, *Proclamation, May 18, 1917*

CONTENTS

OUR SCHOOLS IN WAR TIME — AND AFTER

OUR SCHOOLS IN WAR TIME—
AND AFTER

CHAPTER I

BRINGING THE WAR INTO THE SCHOOLS

The summer of 1917 found America realizing
that the war which it had entered was not going to
be won by the mobilization of an army and a navy,
however strong and efficient they might be. In the
proclamation of Woodrow Wilson the whole nation
was called upon to mobilize with a clear, succinct
purpose of organizing those forces of industry, of
education, of woman power, which are back of every
successful struggle of a nation in peace or in war.
The ready acceptance of the slogan "Win the War
in the Air," with the public clamor for aviation, was
but an indication of the general awakening of the
public to the truth that the war must be won by
the use of forces as yet undeveloped, or undirected
towards national ends.

The mobilization which teaches the saving of
our national resources, which directs the thoughtful
distribution and wise use of our products, which

cultivates the patriotic spirit of service in the boy and girl power of the nation, properly belongs to the field of education, not only in war but in peace. To the schools of America, therefore, the war has come as an opportunity for developing a closer relation between education and life, between life and service.

Our gradual entrance into the war and our distance from the conflict have given us the chance of pausing and surveying the situation before acting, — advantages which were unfortunately denied England and France. At the beginning of the war England apparently almost wrecked her schools, and is slowly repairing the mistakes of hurried action in suspending the attendance laws. France is saving her schools that the nation may go on after the war. *It remains for America to use the war to make better schools.*

The mobilization of our schools is not concerned with the introduction of military drill, whether voluntary or compulsory. It is an experiment in working out the relation of education to war. We are, all of us, empirics in this experiment; there is no body of tradition and theory to help us. The ancient world offers us no parallels; the modern German system throws no light on it. America, equally with the nations of the older world, is a pioneer in the field. This is a novel experience for us who have been originators only of free education in the past or of administrative systems, not of types of new education. Largely what we have to guide us is some experience of France and England in what to avoid. This negative counsel is valuable in restricting our experiments, but is scarcely constructive in its nature. One of its most valuable lessons, however, is to show us that we must not take our schools into the war, as England did, but *bring the war into the schools.*

The fact that the problem is a novel one and that it is experimental does not make it futile. All education is experimental in adapting the individual to his changing environment.

During recent years our schools have had to consider the outside forces of the changing world. It was in 1881 that the first manual-training high school opened its doors under the hostile gaze of incredulity and disapproval. Since then our educational system has been bombarded with essays on the relation of education to life, on practical aspects of education, on vocational guidance, on trade schools, etc. We have only to look at the vastly differentiated courses of our colleges (some of which have lost all trace of the humanities), at the variegated courses in our high schools, at our remodeled elementary courses, to realize that in thirty years the whole attitude of the people towards our schools has undergone a vast change. These changes were regarded as revolutionary at first. But it is no more revolutionary to introduce the war into our schools than it was to introduce the laboratory study of sciences, or agricultural studies, or courses in millinery and home-making, — that is, if we understand the meaning of *war into the schools*.

It is not to be denied that the educational emphasis is different. The student who takes an agricultural course, and thus prepares himself to be a modern efficient farmer, is only indirectly doing work of service to the State. His aim is individual improvement, an advance which results in general benefit to the State; whereas a girl who does Red Cross work in school, or a boy who works in a war garden, benefits the individual through the larger service of collective responsibility in serving the nation directly.

We are not unmindful of the fact that war is a temporary condition, and we must not crowd out the fundamental studies to meet the needs of a temporary environment, however urgent the need may be. In carrying the war into our schools we must emphasize those permanent elements which are as necessary in war as in peace; we must use the war as an opportunity to develop service to the State, — service which may be vitalizing and ennobling, full of purposeful appreciation of collective responsibility.

In our study of the introduction of the war into our schools we may properly shut out discussions of elements which have no educational value. Many of the proposals for the war uses of our schools have been of a haphazard nature, called out by a well-meant desire to meet the emergency. Much of the legislation concerning itself with the employment of school children or of those under compulsory school age has been, and may yet be, harmful. The suggestion of using the schools as recruiting stations has lost value with the operation of the selective draft. Ill-considered proposals to turn over the vocational and manual-training departments to the government for the purpose of making munitions have shown a lack of knowledge of their meager equipment for an industry highly specialized with standard jigs and fixtures. A department store, a clothing factory, a library, or an office building would be about as fit for such a purpose as a school building. The same may be said of the use of our schools as hospitals. Our schools must be retained as educative plants, — training munition workers, if we will, but not making munitions; providing the government with skilled artisans and scientists, but by no means converting their function of education into that of industrial production.

The war work of our schools is more easily planned in those which have technical and vocational departments than in those which contain only the desk and office equipment. Distinctions must be made, too, between schools in agricultural and industrial centers. The experiments made in New York with "farm cadets" show that the country boy has certain advantages over the city boy in all forms of rural and garden employment. We must not expect the same kind of work from the high-school boys and girls in New York City that we may exact from country children of the same age.

The city boy may be needed in emergency office and factory work. Instead of contributing service as a farm cadet, he may become a "coöperator," giving part-time service to industry and to commerce and part time to school, as many of our city boys are now doing.

In dealing with the institution of higher grade we find as many distinctions in service. In the college of the cultural type — the college of individualism — it is the individual who serves the

State, how nobly may be seen in the English universities of Oxford and Cambridge. In the public schools and socialized institutions with vocational work, however, it is the institution which serves. This service of the institution may be classified under two heads. In the case of the elementary schools to some extent, and of the high schools to a greater extent, our war work should be brought into them. In the technical, vocational, and trade schools the institution should reach out towards the war. In the first instance the function of the elementary and secondary school should be to adhere to the purposes for which they were created. The function of the higher technical, vocational, and trade schools should be to prepare the skilled students to take the places of those who are called to military service; to give scientific training, indispensable in war; to assist, through courses for the blind and crippled, in the reëducation of those disabled in war service, — that is, our technical schools may be schools of special preparation and industrial readjustment.

We shall observe, in working out the problem, that we have offered to us by the war an opportunity to make our schools better by bringing education closer to life, not only materially but spiritually. If we have failed to train our youth in coöperation and service to the State in the past, the war gives us a new motive. For to impart skill in use of hand or brain without teaching collective responsibility is to fail in our national duty. To our schools we must look as the agencies which are to carry on the great work of education in service, a noble and purposeful objective for which to work, directing the growth of our children into an efficient and devoted citizenship.

Someone will urge: "The war will soon be over and we shall hardly get started in war service before there will be no need for such service."

Of course those who believe, or at least seem to practice the belief, that the schools are to lag far behind every economic, industrial, and social movement and are to be mere looking-glasses for the workaday world, — such people would not be expected to bring the war into the schools until some historian had written a text setting forth the dates, drawing the battle lines, naming the commanding generals, and picturing the final boundaries determined by some Hague conference. It is such professional obstructionists who make no provision for the millions of our foreign born to learn the English language and American customs through the establishment of up-to-date methods in teaching the adult illiterate. It is such *laissez-faire* persons who allow children to slide out of school unprepared physically, mentally, or vocationally for the life ahead. It is such who insist upon the disciplinary-value idea of subject-worth in the face of modern psychological thought. It is such conservatives who say that agriculture can be taught only on the farm; that it is the business of the factory to teach the trades; that girls may learn to cook from their mothers; that elementary courses in woodworking and freehand drawing constitute vocational training; that algebra, Latin, ancient history, and trigonometry are essential features of the curriculum for training capable stenographers. It is these people who say that "the public schools of America are bulwarks of the nation," and consistently erect bulwarks against every agency which actually reflects the social and economic needs of the day.

But those who believe that the school should study the past and live in the present and strive for a better future will find that the war brings out for the schools not only the lessons of a day, but the needs and opportunities of a decade.

It has been stated that movements or men unresponsive to the present world crisis and failing to meet present needs and opportunities do not deserve to exist. Whether the statement be exactly true or not, it is evident that the up-to-the-minute man or the live school or the progressive industrial establishment or the efficient department of government is responding to the national need in exact proportion to the response made to the needs and opportunities existing before war was declared.

It is this responding power which is testing our men and women, our institutions of government, our industries, and our schools. Nothing makes this clearer than the daily news. We read that since the Railroads War Board has been established, the railroads have increased their operating efficiency 26 per cent, with the result that they are now handling twice the freight and have 75 per cent fewer idle cars; that aëroplane motors are soon to be built as rapidly as a certain well-known automobile can be; that standardized destroyers and merchant ships are to be turned out by the scores; that dyes equal to those formerly imported have been evolved; that prominent men of means have contributed their services to men in authority in Washington; that well-known social workers are on their way to France and Belgium.

All these things and countless others show us how a military necessity has brought out the best

that is within us. And the best of it all is that
there is nothing which we are doing in the way
of making standardized products or in extending
the services of useful men that cannot be permanently useful after the war is over. Our military necessity is teaching us new and permanently
effective standards of making things. Meanwhile,
are the schools of America to fail by not rendering service to a nation in time of need, by not
establishing permanently effective standards in the
making of useful boys and girls, — "boys and girls,"
as Roosevelt puts it, "who realize that they are
a part of Uncle Sam's team"?

The schools and colleges that were alive before
the war began are breathing the breath of life more
deeply now. Those which were asleep are waking
up and not only learning to serve, but through
this service learning to live. A little school in
Vermont in a report on what it has in the way of
war equipment states that it has only ten benches,
but adds that these have been used by sixty boys
who take manual training. A school system which
can be as efficient as that in time of peace may
naturally be expected to state, as it does in response to a recent inquiry: "Our instructor has
been on the job all summer, helping especially
where the boys and girls are working on the

farms or have gardens. He has also organized canning and drying clubs and is giving instruction to different groups of boys."

The university which has extension courses in time of peace naturally has war extension courses. The prominent business man of Massachusetts who for years interested himself in state Y.M.C.A. work would naturally be expected to enlist, as he has, for Y.M.C.A. work in France. Now if the college or institution or individual serves in time of need because of a habit of serving, might it not be equally true that a somnolent individual or school, if once stirred to service, might through such service learn always to serve?

At this time the government of the United States is going to learn how to become efficient. The state colleges of agriculture are testing their former efficiency, — the test being the power to serve. Schools may now learn what it means to be efficient by the service which they may now render. Not an activity is proposed nor a principle of educational practice given in the chapters which follow but should be brought into our schools in times of peace.

We are going to sew now for the Red Cross because it is war time. Later we shall sew for institutions in our community. Now we are going to develop part-time schools because industry needs boys. Later we shall have coöperative courses because boys at work need further schooling. Now we are placing city boys on farms because the farmers need labor. Later we shall place farms on the minds of boys because youth needs contact with nature. Now we have current-events discussions about loans, submarines, aëroplanes, and I. W. W.'s because the government needs support. Later we shall teach the meaning of the same things because thoughtfully trained people are needed by the government. Now we are to teach patriotism and thrift because the nation needs them. Later we shall teach them because they are essential in themselves.

Now we have extension courses in economical cooking for adult women as a war measure. Later we shall have it as a home measure. Now we are bringing adult women into the schools to receive instruction with their children. Later we shall do the same thing because it is the only sensible procedure under any and all conditions. Now we think in terms of reëducation of disabled soldiers because of the immediate need of helping these honored men. Later we shall turn what we have learned to do for these men into better provisions for making self-supporting our crippled and blinded children who are now in dependent institutions being made still more dependent by the very nature of the poor apology for vocational training which is given them. Now we have clearly before us the need for industrial education because the government is crying for workers. Later we shall see the need for industrial education because those who are to work in the industries need it. Now we hold a child-labor law before youth tempted by industry. Later we shall endeavor to hold before youth better opportunities for vocational, physical, and mental training in our schools as an inducement to stay in them.

What are the schools and colleges going to do about it all? Certainly they will not intentionally injure the cause of education by starting ill-developed ideas of war service. But the desire to avoid the bad should not by any means imply inaction. This is the psychological moment for all of us to justify our very existence as individuals or as parts of an institution or a movement. One could only pity a school man who recently said: " Really, I am envious of some of my colleagues. They have something to do at this time, while the subject which I am teaching can make no contribution."

There has never been a time in our school life when taxpayers, boards of apportionment, women's clubs, state granges, boards of trade, could be made more interested in having the schools broaden out along lines of continuation-school and part-time work, differentiated courses in our high schools, physical-training courses, evening courses for adult illiterates, thrift measures and school savings, teaching of current events, more practical science work, teaching of agriculture, unit courses in household arts, and a score of other things which the school men of America say they want and which they are always saying " the public will not stand for."

Shall we let the golden opportunity for enrichment pass until after the war, when cities will most certainly preach and practice poverty?

Now is the time to evaluate our school subjects, to bring in the new if they are worth while, to scrap the old if they do not stand the test of national needs. If a community will not "stand for" cooking when the H. C. L. rises like a specter before our doors, it will never vote for household arts after the war. If a city school favorably located near the open country will not now extend its educational program to include community gardening when prices of farm products are excessive, it will hardly broaden out when the crisis of our material needs is over. If a state will not line up with the Federal Board of Vocational Education for national aid for its vocational schools when its industries are crying for trained youth, it will never move forward in time of a normal demand. If we do not reorganize our schools to bring in the best while we may, we shall in all probability be required in the near future to discard some things which we have, without having any opportunity to develop the new things which we have stated in our conventions and teachers' institutes that we earnestly desire. World conditions challenge our schools. What is their program?

CHAPTER II

WAR AND COMMUNITY USES OF OUR SCHOOLS

An evaluating test for each of our school subjects has at last been found. *The test is the capacity of the subject to respond to a national need or a national ideal.* In many instances of the countries concerned in this great war the schools as a whole have amply justified their existence, and many of the subjects taught have stood through this world emergency the acid test of meeting national needs. The scientific and efficiency spirit of Germany is reflected in the posters spread over Berlin : " Send your cherry, peach, and plum seeds to the school-house with your children," seeds being used for making fat and oil. The spirit of France has been reflected, as will be seen in the following pages, in the work of the teachers and the children for the preservation of that wonderful nationalism of France. The schools of England are reshaping themselves — in fact, are being remade — as a result of the shortcomings set forth by the war.

The schools of America are to go forward. Patriotism now has a new meaning. The principal from his school platform has opportunity for announcements and talks other than those dealing with routine matters. The cooking teacher has opportunity to develop new recipes adapted to present needs. The teacher of history may redraw almost every day the map of Europe. The teacher of manual training may substitute problems in concrete for those requiring high-priced wood materials. The school buildings near soldiers' camps may, like the Washington (D. C.) buildings, be opened for educational purposes for soldiers, that they may take up general or special educational work. Teachers of English may have their pupils study President Wilson's messages of state as models of English composition and expressions of American democracy.

The opportunity is before the schools and the children. There are in our school system three elements which may be of use in war: the building itself with its equipment, the school population of boy and girl power, and the teaching force.

In England, during the first year of the war, all three were called into requisition. Within a few months over 1000 school buildings were in temporary military use, and even on August 1, 1916, 180 elementary- and 20 secondary-school buildings were still occupied for war work, — for hospitals,

billeting of troops, housing of munition workers, etc.,
— the number of children displaced being 129,855.
In many cases the use was expected to be temporary, but many buildings have been retained permanently. The children whose schooling was thus
interrupted, when too young for employment, generally drifted aimlessly into juvenile delinquency,
while those older, although below the established
employment age, went to farms and munition factories. That is, the taking away of the school
building was concomitant with the suspension of
restrictions on age of employment and hours of
labor. The children of the prosperous class were
likewise affected by the departure of over 50 per
cent of the teachers for military service.

These many interruptions in the carrying on of
educational work were the result of the short-war
fallacy; they were emergency measures adopted to
meet a condition which it was generally supposed
would last but a few months. When, however, it
was realized by statesmen and the public that the
interference with education and the suspension of
laws regulating employment were resulting in ir-
reparable injury to health and morals of an employed child population under 13 years of age of
150,000, and an idle younger population variously
estimated at from 200,000 to 300,000, corrective

measures were adopted. American schools must learn from English experience what to avoid. There are many legitimate uses of schools which England is now employing; and the warnings of interested English educators should keep our legislatures and municipalities from breaking down the compulsory-education laws or converting our schools into industrial plants. Our aim, as previously stated, should be to bring the war to the school curriculum for educational purposes, not to take the schools into the war, losing sight of their definite function.

In France, at the outbreak of the war, many of the school buildings were requisitioned, and 30,000 teachers were called to the colors. The hardship to the young resulting from this patriotic sacrifice was met as far as possible by the generosity of private citizens who gave rooms or buildings for classes, and by professional men, too old for service, who volunteered to carry on the work of teaching. France was swift to realize that education must be carried on at all costs. In districts near the fighting line schools were of necessity transformed into hospitals, often with a staff of women teachers temporarily acting as nurses and attendants; but it has been the policy of the department of public instruction to regard this service as temporary, and the teachers as conscripted for education.

The trying circumstances under which the schools have been carried on, serving nobly during the term after hours and during vacations, make their achievements a record of honor. In the country districts where all the local officials were mobilized, the teacher became the sole agent of government, making out passports, requisitions, relief lists, etc., procuring food, operating a public kitchen, acting as postmaster, doing guard duty, and rendering numberless other services to the community. One of the first tasks of the primary schools was to undertake entire care of children left without adequate protection. In country districts the teachers were, in default of newspapers, the dispensers of official information, explaining government loans and giving talks on the progress of the war. Thus the entire village was brought into the schoolhouse, which became the real center of the community.

In the United States and Canada the schools may well copy some of the measures initiated in Europe. That we are 3000 miles from the actual battleground ought, for the present, to keep us from considering any lowering of educational bars or from converting our buildings into purposes other than educational. Europe advises us that such transformation is of an emergency nature and only to be made under stress of an invasion.

It is the purpose of this chapter to consider some general uses of our buildings, our equipment (including the teaching force), and the activities of our pupils, which have been made in the past two or three years, excluding and reserving for the most part for later discussion the introduction of war work in manual-training, domestic-arts, and domestic-science courses, and the part-time agricultural labor.

An important use of our schools, and one which should be made more general throughout the country, is that of a distributing center for government pamphlets, information cards, etc. In New York City the various welfare committees appointed by Mayor Mitchel designated the public schools as mediums through which to circulate papers on "safety first," fire prevention, uses of various food products, etc., and thus reach the families of the vast foreign population through their children. The city's pledges of national loyalty to be signed by adults were circulated by the pupils shortly after the declaration of war. Wider publicity can be given to federal regulations, tax measures, employment modifications, etc., by the distribution of notices to pupils of upper grades, following the explanation by the teacher. While our people as a whole read, though hastily, the newspapers morning and evening, and may find in them all governmental measures, it is nevertheless true that we shall be assured of a wider distribution of information by using the pupil as the carrier of it to the home. In England the schools, as well as the Boy Scouts organization, have served as national distributing agencies for war-office notices, Parliamentary information, and agricultural propaganda.

A portion of a letter from Sir Robert Blair, chairman of the Education Committee of the London County Council, to Superintendent Maxwell of New York City, in May, 1917, calls attention to the service of the schools in this connection.

War has come upon us so unexpectedly that our people not only did not understand the true position but on the whole knew very little about the causes which had led to the outbreak. The public press, bookstalls, and the public libraries were considerably augmented by books and pamphlets on the subject, and it was a natural prompting that gave rise to the issue to the schools of a considerable number of documents, memoranda, and pamphlets. These circulars and pamphlets were mostly all issued within the first year of the war. The first phase of the pamphlets is historical, while the second became economical. The economical phase in its first stages was concentrated on war savings for the purpose of war loans and in anticipation, by the provision of " nest eggs," of the dislocation that might occur at the end of the war. In its later stages — within the last six months — the economical phase has been directed chiefly to economy in food, owing to the menace of the submarine campaign.

A further use of the school population in hours outside the daily session is that of giving help in taking a census. In England school teachers and pupils did most of the work of compiling the National Register, a card census of inhabitants. To some extent similar work has been done in the United States, such as the taking of the agricultural census in fifty-six counties (no census was taken for the counties of Hamilton, Kings, Queens, Richmond, and New York) in the state of New York in April, 1917. Under the joint auspices of the State Food Supply Commission and the State Education Department a survey was ordered of the agricultural resources of the state and of the requirements for increased production, the details of which were worked out at Ithaca at the State College of Agriculture. Through the appointed county enumerators, instructions were transmitted to the various school districts.

The actual work of this census was begun in most counties on April 23, the records being practically all obtained by April 25, the teachers and pupils in each district, assisted when necessary

by other persons, procuring the original facts from
farmers and making the summaries for their school
districts. From these records the state was within
ten days furnished with the complete amount of
seed and live stock wanted by farmers and for sale
by farmers; with the statements of the transportation difficulties; with the itemized needs of labor,
fertilizer, and spray materials; and with the complete enumeration of the state, — people, land, and
live stock.

Such work by pupils might well become an
established yearly activity. The practice of gathering and tabulating information has an obvious
arithmetical value; and the interest developed in
investigating the resources of the community has
an educational significance which should keep us
from limiting it to emergency periods.

The comparative table on page 26 (one of thirteen
developed out of the census) not only illustrates
facts which the children obtained, but also shows
the magnitude of the work they undertook.

One of the best community uses of the school is
as a center for instruction in conserving food products. With the absolute shortage of the world's
food supply, Americans must anticipate this shortage in coming seasons and revert to the preserving
methods of their grandparents, — measures fallen

into disuse in crowded cities because of lack of storage room and the ease with which the fresh products have been obtained, whatever the season.

ACRES OF CROPS IN 56 COUNTIES IN NEW YORK WITH
COMPARISONS FOR THE SAME COUNTIES IN 1909

CROP	ACRES (U.S. Census, 1909)	ACRES GROWN IN 1916	ACRES EXPECTED TO BE GROWN IN 1917
Corn for grain . . .	511,339	336,543	495,469
Corn for silo	259,082	362,413	422,867
Oats	1,302,041	1,102,004	1,250,346
Barley	79,955	92,422	111,634
Buckwheat	286,128	257,911	300,090
Winter wheat . . .	289,126	344,278	387,813
Spring wheat . . .	289,126	12,373	32,425
Rye	130,449	114,691	120,239
Field beans	115,695	194,053	275,790
Alfalfa	35,343	160,985	181,912
Other hay	4,737,326	4,073,333	3,963,678
Cabbage	33,770	38,898	68,890
Potatoes	390,552	305,649	382,840
Canning-factory crops ⎫		44,098	60,155
Other vegetables and ⎬	131,686		
garden . . . . ⎭		58,340	71,833
Miscellaneous crops .	21,843	35,056	40,895
Apples	281,061		346,633
Cherries	4,211		12,414
Peaches	15,340		50,149
Pears	13,378		36,802
Plums	5,742		8,569
Vineyards	52,999		52,350
Small fruit	22,388		28,171
Total	8,719,454		8,701,964

Even villages which have no gas supply may follow the example of cities and towns in using the school kitchen, already installed as part of a domestic-science equipment or newly supplied by popular subscription, as a community canning center. Certainly schools are as well adapted for the purpose as department stores and Young Women's Christian Associations, which have been leaders in the movement.

The teaching of methods of preserving is primarily the function of a school, and every suitable school building should be employed for it. The old-fashioned preserving meant time, drudgery, expense, quantities of sugar, and doubtful results. A demonstration of the newer methods and the opportunity for community canning should be given by the school to the neighborhood. Community canning induces a far more effective conservation of food than is possible for the individual kitchen. Few households can afford to buy and store the vast kettles, the perfected drying and dehydrating ovens, which can be included in the equipment of a school teaching the scientific preserving of food and vegetables. As this is done almost wholly in the summer, it would not interfere with the term's work of the pupils and, in fact, offers the high-school girls an excellent opportunity to assist in civic service of a most practical nature. In the summer of 1917 Seattle maintained 20 centers for home-economics teaching for adult women, the government bulletin "How to Select Food" being used as a textbook.

There have been wholesome experiments in community canning in Lakewood, and in Bernards Township, New Jersey. In the latter in each school was an experienced teacher to supervise the work of preserving performed by high-school girls of the neighborhood, the fruits and vegetables being sold by the townspeople to the school or brought by them to be conserved by coöperative canning for their own use in the future. This service of the girls was on an equality with that of the boys who belonged to the agricultural army. In Kansas City the surplus garden products canned by schoolgirls were used for the school lunches.

England's schools now have "open days" on which parents may be admitted to receive the instruction given to the children in the economical cooking of the food which the food controller's instructions show is likely to be available for general consumption; also (quoting from a letter from Sir Robert Blair of the London County Council, May 30, 1917) the responsible mistresses of the evening schools and the domestic-economy staff

employed in these schools are organizing traveling
kitchens in 29 boroughs within the county. These
traveling kitchens form practically a demonstration
set of apparatus by which the simplest forms of
cookery can be shown to 100 or 200 people. The
demonstrations are well attended, and the people
in small villages thus have the opportunity of
those in larger settlements to learn from experts
methods of making palatable the food products less
well understood.

It may be urged that community canning has its
place outside cities of the first class. New York
City certainly cannot be held to be the center of
an agricultural district, and yet valuable experiments in food conservation are being made there.
One is concerned primarily with the prevention of
waste. Of the thousands of pounds of perishable
vegetables and fruit which are brought each day to
the produce piers, much is prohibited from being
sold to retailers because of injuries received in transportation. When more than 20 per cent has been
injured, it has not paid wholesalers to salvage the
uninjured portion. As a result, a ruinous quantity
of produce has gone to waste, often being dumped
in the harbor for want of better disposal. The
loss as estimated by the board of health has been
225,000 pounds a week.

To save this food by making quick use of it, in July, 1917, Mayor Mitchel's Committee of Women on National Defense opened a conservation kitchen in a disused school building in the Williamsburg Bridge section. Here the uncertain quantity of vegetables salvaged from the produce piers was brought to the school, picked over, and sterilized, partly by paid labor, partly by the volunteer labor of members of the Women's University Club and other organizations, or city women who were willing to contribute their labor in the cause of food saving. This work was aided by the State Food Supply Commission and New York's board of health, one of whose inspectors passed judgment on the food used in the canning and drying experiments. The salvaged food was brought from the piers to the kitchens by Boy Scouts, ubiquitously useful in any public undertaking. If it had not been that the kitchen was opened in vacation, the school population would have had its share of work to do. To this kitchen any woman might go to be taught processes or actually to can produce.

While it was not possible to use all the produce brought in, even by keeping the kitchen as full of workers as space would allow and cooking as much as 480 gallons of food at a time, the work in this old school building is illustrative of what can be done in community centers to eliminate waste, and is a vital example of the efficient use of a school building in vacation. The cost in this case was met by special contributions of organizations and individuals. But in smaller places this work might be maintained by the town itself on a less elaborate scale. Such work should not be limited to the war period. It is a practical and efficient plan for all time.

The continued war will undoubtedly increase not only the price but the scarcity of cotton and woolen goods. Where it has hitherto not paid to make over clothing repeatedly because of the cheapness and ease with which new garments and children's wear have been procured, it is now important to understand thrifty saving of all kinds of fabrics and apparel.

Home-economics women of Berkeley, California, aided in collecting and making over old clothing. In Portland, Oregon, a cleaner and dyer took as his bit of service the cleaning and disinfecting of all the clothing which was remade by the school children.

In England's county schools there have been held exhibitions of thrift, to show children when and how economies can be practiced. Some of the examples shown under the heading of "Utilization of Waste Material" were as follows: old linen collars and cuffs made into baggage labels, window cleaners made from pieces of old gloves, house slippers made from old felt hats, mops made of bits of rags fastened to a nail. Ways were shown of making use of scraps of wool left over from knitting, the wasting of an inch of wool being regarded as treasonable in the country's shortage; methods of refooting stockings were also displayed, as well as many uses for pieces of worn table and bed linen and old carpets.

In times of normal plenty such exhibitions would not attract attention, but no greater evidence of the reduced state of a nation at war can be had than the seriousness with which these exhibitions of household thrift have been viewed by the population. A clipping from a newspaper of rural England requests that children go into the pastures and pick from the bushes the bits of wool which the sheep have rubbed off.

For several years, at least, there will be high prices and scarcity of materials. Our children must be taught the necessity of preventing waste of fabrics as well as of food. Millions of dollars worth of cotton and wool have been destroyed in military and munition use. But it is not only because war conditions have made material scarce and high that thrift in their use must be insisted upon in every

Old-fashioned methods of preserving must again prevail. There is educational value in community conservation. Montclair (New Jersey) boys made community evaporators, having a capacity of from five to eight bushels of fruit a day, at a cost of only $10

A mowing machine is a problem in high-school mechanics, and these farm cadets of New York State see, perhaps for the first time, a use for it

A day's outing for a purpose. Albany and Troy (New York) orphan-asylum boys on their way to "do their bit" in the currant fields

A lesson in service geography. Boys from Albany and Troy (New York) picking currants, near Hudson (New York), which were preserved in Yonkers Trades School for shipment to France

household; we must remember that billions of dollars will be required to pay for this war and each household will be required to make its contribution. Expenditures in every direction must be curbed and the wise disposition of every dollar must be made. A year or so ago the Bankers Association of America launched a campaign for thrift teaching. We were then told that, as individuals, we must save for the future. The present high cost of living shows that we are obliged to save in the present in order to live in the present, but the future will tell us to save in order that we, as a nation, may pay for the war.

Many community services may be rendered during the war by the principal of a school. He may, as has been done, organize patriotic meetings, enlisting the aid of the churches and arousing the interest of chambers of commerce, civic clubs, and women's clubs in the Red Cross, the Liberty Loan, and school war gardens. His assembly exercises may be made vital through talks to the pupils on opportunities for war service; through platform recognition of boys and girls rendering special farm, garden, Red Cross, and food-conservation help; by placing on a conspicuous bulletin a roll of honor of graduates and students engaged in such work; by keeping the school in touch with graduates who are enlisted in the army and navy by reading their letters to the school and sending school packets to them. He may advise economy in the use of foods and clothing, the elimination of expenditures in soda water, ice cream, and gum, and the sacrifice of pleasure for national ends. He may urge the use of savings in the purchase of government bonds and war-savings certificates. Where the school has been raising money for pictures or a phonograph, he may suggest that the funds raised be used for the purchase of one or more government bonds, to be held by the school as an asset until the close of the war, when the bond may be sold and the money used for its original purpose of buying the phonograph or pictures. In the case of some private secondary schools, and large public schools like the Washington Irving and De Witt Clinton high schools, New York, the pupils and teachers have subscribed money and given entertainments for the purchase of an ambulance, the gift of the school to the American Expeditionary Force. In one New York City school, through the efforts of a student organization, Liberty Loan bonds to the amount of $479,800 were sold.

The principal in country districts should make himself fully informed of the details of the federal farm-loan plan, the sources of available seed supply, the posters and bulletins of nation and state regarding the mobilization of schools and colleges, and, of course, he should be especially active in encouraging the home-garden projects.

A correspondent in the London *Times*, June 14, 1917, writing of that indispensable teaching of thrift in household affairs, of making the present generation of young girls intelligently self-sufficient in domestic and industrial life, cries, " This brings us to the crux of the whole situation: Who shall teach the teachers? " The government and state bulletins on food production and conservation, the literature sent out by state councils of defense and public safety on improved methods of preserving, the pronouncements by banking houses on thrift measures and means of attaining them, the Boy Scouts, Y.M.C.A. and Y.W.C.A. leaflets on war gardens and food economies are, in America, beginning to answer this question.

Assuredly the war places an additional burden on the teachers and gives them a new opportunity for educating the pupils. A teacher does not have to belong to the department of domestic arts and science to organize Red Cross circles nor to instruct girls in food conservation. A ten-minute talk each morning by teacher or pupils, before the opening of school, with discussion on such topics as " Why a man with a hundred dollars to invest should buy a Liberty Bond," " New occupations open to women because of the war," " The reason for the scarcity of certain products," " Home substitutes for various manufactured necessities," and many others suggested by new conditions should be very helpful.

An unusually significant experiment known as the " War Savings " movement has been made in English schools. On May 5, 1916, the Board of Education issued a circular asking for the assistance of local education authorities in making known through public elementary schools the facilities afforded by the issue of War Savings certificates. Then, with the coöperation of these authorities and teachers, special lessons were given on the subject, and copies of a leaflet explaining the purpose of the War Savings Association were widely distributed to the parents through their children. As a result a large number of War Savings associations were formed in direct connection with the schools. The success of the movement is evident from the records given in the report of the Board of Education for 1915–1916. In one populous midland county the great majority of the schools have established associations; in another, a northern county, some 70 per cent of the schools

have taken part and record nearly 10,000 subscribers. In one midland town a school of about
1400 children purchased certificates to the value
of £585 in three months. But it is not only
in large schools that the pupils have contributed
generously; a remote little school in a northern
county, with only 10 children on its register, has
10 subscribers to its credit and has saved £35,
buying 43 certificates.

In view of the fact that successive issues of bonds
must be made by the United States and other governments of the world, this method of making subscription to the war loan popular is worthy of
attention. The public schools have, as never before,
the opportunity of showing the practical value of
investing, in peace as well as in war time, in government and other bonds. Pupils should realize
the difference between money invested in a way
to be beneficial not only to the investor but to
his state and country, and money invested in
ordinary channels.

New York State teachers had an opportunity
similar to those of England. The Regents of the
University of the state of New York gave formal
approval of a plan by which teachers throughout
the public schools of the state could aid the Liberty
Loan committee of the Federal Reserve Bank in

giving instruction and information about the second Liberty Loan. A special committee was appointed by the Board of Regents to act in a supervisory capacity to keep the State Education Department in touch with the large financial interests conducting the loan. The secretary to Commissioner Finley, as the representative of the Regents and the State Education Department, was assigned for temporary services in the office of the Loan committee.

The program in brief was to have the teachers act as agents for subscriptions for the Liberty Loan. They distributed blanks to pupils in the school, who in turn took them to their parents. They were encouraged to subscribe themselves. They did not handle any money or checks, but turned the subscription blanks over to the local bank, which was, of course, in direct touch with the Loan committee in New York City.

A primer of instruction for teachers was prepared in the simplest possible terms. As published by the Publicity Bureau of the United States Treasury Department it was called " A Source Book of the Second Liberty Loan." This primer explained in detail the nature of the bonds, their security, and the terms and prices; it described the nature of bond markets in general, the sources from which interest is paid, the previous records of United States bonds, and all other matter which was of value in elementary financial instruction. It was all set forth in a way which was very helpful not only in assisting in the sale of bonds but in the larger sense of furthering instruction in bonds, interest, discounts, etc., in connection with work in arithmetic. And in what better way could arithmetical instruction be furthered?

It is highly probable that this plan of informing the public relative to government issues of bonds and certificates, initiated in New York, will extend to all parts of the country in connection with the next Loan campaign.

How the responsibility of the teacher has been met in France is in part suggestive. The teachers have collected large funds to finance the enterprise of caring for thousands of families of Belgian and French refugees. They also collected from the civilian population several millions of francs, the teachers taxing themselves according to a fixed schedule. They have been especially successful in bringing to light for investment stores of hidden gold in the homes of provincial savers. Surprising results have been attained through their persistent, methodical propaganda. In one large provincial town, after a talk to the older pupils by

the mistress of the school, in four days an amount
equal to 7200 francs was brought in. In the same
school the following composition was given out to
the pupils as part of an admission examination
in penmanship.

THE GOLD OF FRANCE [1]

France has need of its gold to defend its invaded territory. It is a sacred duty for every French man and woman,
rich or poor, to send to the coffers of the State the hundreds
of louis from their strong boxes, the few louis hidden in
the linen chest at home, even the single louis in the children's toy bank. To keep in one's own possession, self-
ishly, the money which could serve our dear France is a
crime against patriotism. So, little girls, do not hesitate
to break open your banks, even if they have only a half
louis inside, and gladly take in exchange the note which
the Bank of France will give you. More than that, in your
vacation in the country, set yourselves to get grandmother
to empty her stocking, — she is sometimes rather stingy
with her money. But you know well enough how to coax
those who love you when you want a toy, or ornament, or
bonbons. Use your influence with your grandparents now,
so that they will bring into the public treasury the gold
of France. In this way you will have contributed to the
coming victory that we are all hoping for, you will have
helped our brave soldiers to clear away the German whose
presence defiles our land. Go, then, all of you! Hunt out
all the money that is lying idle. It is for France!

[1] Edouard Petit, De l'école à la guerre, p. 175. Paris, 1916.

Thus the schools have worked to bring to light the hoarded gold of thrifty peasants for investment in the national loan.

Tangible as this service of the teachers has been to France, of greater importance has been their work of making clear to the villages the cause of France. In November, 1914, the Department of Public Instruction sent out an appeal to the professional and volunteer teachers in the secondary schools, saying that the schools must adapt their program to the duties and needs created by the hostilities.

The teachers will do their best to make the schools serve in the national defense. In the evenings the old men, the youths, and the women will gather together, and the teachers will tell them the news, explain things that happen, speak to them of patriotism, and read to them from our writers whose pages are inspired with the glorious deeds of our history past and present.

It is reported that in the girls' schools in France war has changed the whole aspect of education. History, geography, lectures on literature, subjects for literary composition or moral instruction, — in fact everything, — is treated from the point of view of country and of patriotic duty. In music practically nothing is sung but the " Marseillaise," the " Chant du Depart," and the national songs of the Allies.

Reading is confined often to official military orders and reports, while drawings are usually of war material or characters.

It is no less the duty of our teachers to make clear to their pupils the " cause " of America. Soon after the opening of the European war a United States senator traveled through the belligerent countries. His articles on Europe at war commented caustically on the ignorance of the English working people of the cause of the war, and of the purpose for which the Allies were fighting. An article on America at war could truthfully contain like criticism of a considerable portion of our population.

Shortly after the United States entered the war a teacher in one of our largest city high schools, where a large proportion of the pupils are of either foreign birth or foreign parentage, asked 200 pupils of from 14 to 18 years to write a brief statement of what they considered to be the cause of America's entrance into the war. While these answers covered an incredible range of inaccuracy, not one showed an understanding of the events which led to the declaration of April, 1917. " Congress has declared war so that the rich folks can get richer," " We are at war because this is a rich man's country," predominated as replies. When asked what a citizen owed his country in return for political and religious freedom, students replied in as vague and cynical a way as to the first question.

To combat this ignorance of national motives the teacher distributed copies of President Wilson's address of April 2, with the ostensible purpose of analyzing it as an exercise in argument and exposition, — a study which finally resulted in enabling these students to make intelligent, if occasionally unsympathetic, answers to questions regarding the nation's action and policy.

Now to residents of favored parts of the country where the population is English speaking and largely American born, inheriting American ideals and traditions, the ignorance of these high-school pupils seems exceptional, but educators know from experiments made in colleges and secondary institutions that the majority of students are not intelligent on modern events of national significance, any more than is the average worker. Nearly all high schools have in their curriculum the study of current events, whether in history or oral English courses. It is the duty of the teacher to use the study in such a manner as to obtain a patriotic reaction to the topics presented and discussed, and in this manner to make clear why we are fighting and what we are fighting for.

Out of this war we must obtain a new spirit of patriotism. Now is the time to strike. Events depicted in the daily press show how great is the need. In this connection the Council of Defense of Connecticut, in an effective campaign working through the schools, states in a recent publication:

The war is bound to have a deep influence on American life and thought, and we should be watchful to direct this into right channels. The country is shot through and through with the one-sided philosophy that the State is an institution to be leaned upon and filched from, but not to be served. The schools should train the children in the fundamental contract between citizen and State. The idea of mutuality should be developed. The State owes duties to the citizen, but the citizen owes reciprocal duties to the State.

In September, 1914, as soon after the declaration of war as military and agricultural conditions would permit the schools to open, the French Minister of Public Instruction sent an official circular to all of the schools. He stated that the first lesson in every school should be devoted to France: to its present danger and its heroic resistance; to the ideals of humanity and justice for which she fought; to the memory of the valor of her soldiers; to the justice of her cause. He desired to make certain at the earliest possible moment that every school child in France take his part spiritually and intellectually in the epic conflict which France was waging for right and justice.

His decree outlining the first lesson for every child of France expresses so clearly the French attitude and feeling that the following free rendering of the circular letter is well worth reading.

The *lycées*, colleges, and public schools are about to open everywhere except where the superior need of improvised hospitals in school buildings caring for our glorious wounded renders this impossible.

I decree that on the opening day in every city and in every class the first words of the teacher to the pupils shall be designed to bring the hearts of the pupils into accord with the sacred struggle in which our armies are engaged.

Throughout the entire country at the same hour the sons of France shall pay respect to the spirit of their nation and shall pay tribute to the heroism of those who are pouring out their blood for liberty, justice, and human right.

The words of the teachers on this occasion should be simple and to the point. They should be adapted to the age of their hearers, some of whom are children, some youths. Each of our schools has sent its quota of combatants to the firing line, — professors, teachers, or pupils ; the words of the teacher to the class should call forth the noble remembrance of the dead, in order to exalt their example and engrave it forever in the memory of the children. Moreover, in its broad lines, calmly, clearly, they should tell the causes of the war, — the aggression without excuse, — and how before the civilized world, France, eternal champion of progress and right, has been compelled to prepare herself, with her valiant allies, to repel the assault of the modern barbarians.

The furious conflict which we are carrying insistently to victory adds each day to the glory of our soldiers a thousand deeds of heroism from which the teacher may take the best part of this lesson. He should prefer these supreme models of action to the vain repetition of phrases, in order to make a fit impression on the minds of the children.

A vivid recollection of this first school hour ought to remain imprinted forever in the spirit of the pupil, who is the citizen of to-morrow. The teacher who has known how to make this impression will remain worthy of the confidence of the republic.

America too will have its lesson sheets, and a most timely one on " Lessons of the Great War in the Classroom " has been prepared for teachers of history by the National Board for Historical Service (Washington, D.C.) with the distinct purpose of suggesting certain aspects of history, ancient and modern, which have gained a new interest in the light of the great war. The following excerpts are extremely suggestive of special opportunities and obligations for teachers in school service:

There is the duty of keeping, for teacher and for pupil, the habit of at least trying to see things as they really were and are. . . . Every great war is fought not merely by armies and navies, but by the governments at home which direct the fighting forces. . . . No one can take an intelligent part in a great conflict for the safety of democracy under an orderly system of international law unless he is really interested in and knows something about other nations than his own. . . . There is some connection between the conditions which made the valleys of the Tigris and Euphrates one of the great seats of ancient civilization and those which are making Mesopotamia to-day one of the chief theaters of the great war. . . . This terrible catastrophe, with its wholesale destruction of the finest products of human civilization, its life and death struggle between opposing nations and opposing ideals, has seemed a reason for thinking not less but more of the great mysterious forces which brought about the rise and decline of the ancient empire. . . . Great campaigns are again carried on where Xenophon marched with his famous Ten Thousand, where Alexander the Great led his armies to the conquest of the East. . . . The opportunity must now be seized to study the whole of Europe and its influence on and connections with the rest of the world. . . . Some account should be given of the way in which the ruling class in Prussia has been able to use science, modern business methods, and social legislation in the service of the military state. . . . War is the business not only of governments but of the nation as a whole, and there are few kinds of human activity which do not have some relation to its success or failure. . . . We are fighting partly, indeed, to defend international law on the high seas, but partly also to make *the world*, not merely America, "safe for democracy."

Teachers are recognized as the instructing force of America. If they are not, who is? If the country sorely needs clear, definite, authentic information on the situation of the world and our own position as a belligerent power, who is to give it if not the teachers? It is they who must inform and arouse. It is they who ought to participate in a speaking campaign which should be as deep as the danger, as wide as the country, and as high as the patriotic spirit of the people. They should be distributing agents for printed material which analyzes the subject, and should be able to refer to the best and most available authorities and to put before pupils and the public the texts of the most important speeches, diplomatic notes, and other approved material to back up statements of fact.

Strange as it may seem, it is the children's convictions which take effect not only when as children they carry word to their parents but also when they come out of childhood into adult life.

Was the boy in the New York high school right when he said, " It is a Wall Street war"? Are our enemies justified in charging us with the same motives of self-interest and the abasement of other nations which animated themselves? Are we really at war for conquest or seizure, or for the benefit of commerce, or for defense against aggressions that have not yet been made? And is it a dollar war for bankers and ammunition makers?

It is to answer these and other questions that a systematic effort to inform and arouse the American people should be taken up and carried into effect by public-school teachers, having in mind that the most effective and most important work may be done in the classroom in connection with lessons in civics and history. To wait for text-books on the present European war is to wait until it is over. To wait to put the study of the present war into a course of study in its chronological sequence is to wait until the next generation of children come upon the stage. No, now is the time for our schools to include the teaching of the war and to discuss officially proposed peace plans, when the street is alive with soldiers, when the newspapers display huge headlines and the bill-boards are covered with recruiting posters, when magazines furnish helpful material for teachers, and when the whole world is charged with feeling.

The National Security League (New York City) has outlined a plan for public addresses and lectures, and it has printed a little book entitled "Wake Up, America." The following topics have been selected from an outline furnished by this league:

Foreign military systems and international relations.

Spirit of the American people as shown in our history of liberty and democracy.

Causes of the war between the United States and Central Powers.

First two and one-half years of the war in relation to the principles of the foreign policy of the United States.

Universal military training and service as now provided by Congress.

Organization and work of the army and navy: selection; supplying needs.

General military preparations in the country at large: materials, transportation, and public finance.

Duty of the citizen in relation to obligations of all citizens as an offset to benefits of citizenship.

Service outside of military and naval; as, for example, the munition work, transportation, building of ships and machinery, farming, etc.

Faithfulness of foreign-born citizens.

Need of efficiency and economy in local, municipal, and state governments.

Description of modern warfare as defining the immediate task of the American people in regard to organization and action of the various services; as, for example, men in the trenches, health protection, Red Cross, etc.

Accessories; for instance, patriotic music and recitations, flag marches, and parades.

Illustrative material, such as maps and charts illustrating the problems of recruiting; slides and movies; posters in public places; exhibitions of foreign posters.

These topics as outlined here are not sufficiently related to the actual conflict. They are excellent from the formal point of view, but they fail to get at the center of living interest in the vital present moment of history. Often when it has been asked of the children in France: "What are you studying?" "What are they teaching you?" the answer has been: "The war, madam." "The war, monsieur." And if the question was taken up with the teacher, the answer has been:

By means of our war map on which is marked the present position of the French and German troops, the particular spot in the line in which the parents of our boys and girls are fighting, we teach not only current history, but in the most vital way geography and many related subjects.

By means of our use of great contemporary political documents, by the speeches of Viviani, Deschanel, Ribot, and the other statesmen, by the famous orders of Joffre, Pétain, and our military leaders, by the interpretation of the war by our great philosophers, — we teach in the most vital way the need of the country, the ideals of France, and much of the history of France. By reason of the war work instituted in every school as part of the regular curriculum, we teach commercial geography, economics, and many branches of science as they are actually related to human life and experience, and not in the abstract manner in which they are treated in the textbooks.

Mr. Albert Sarraut, Minister of Public Instruction in France in 1914–1915, said in a public address:

If there remains in the schools of France a single teacher who has not been profoundly touched by the war and who goes about his usual occupation of teaching in the same way that he did prior to August 2, 1914, teaching the same subjects in the same way, doing only the ordinary, familiar school tasks, whose work has not been entirely transformed and inspired by the war, we have yet to hear of him or her, and we do not believe that such exists.

It is inevitable that many of our school subjects will change their emphasis after the war. To some teachers the awakening will be cruel, to others a blessing in the form of new opportunity.

CHAPTER III

THE FIELD FOR INDUSTRIAL AND TRADE SCHOOLS

For ten years a group of men in America have been trying to convince Congress that we should set up a national program of secondary vocational education. As a precedent we have had a system of agricultural and mechanic-arts education of collegiate grade in existence for the last fifty years. But we have had in the past no system of national aid for promoting and maintaining a type of vocational education in agriculture, mechanic arts, and home-making, which would reach a much larger clientele than could possibly be touched through any land-grant college system. It has been an up-hill fight to get Congress to see the importance of providing vocational education for industrial workers. Bill after bill was introduced providing for national aid. These bills defined vocational education as including all types of industrial, commercial, agricultural, and home-making schools, between the upper grammar grades and the college, whose controlling purpose is to fit for specific profitable employments and which receive pupils 14 years of age and over.

President Wilson in his second inaugural message called the country's attention definitely to the fact that a vocational-education bill was before Congress and that it ought to receive favorable consideration, not only on the grounds of educational advantages contained in the bill, but also on the grounds that it fitted in with a national economic and industrial policy.

Perhaps the measure would have met the fate of its predecessors if war had not been declared. Friends of the measure feared lest discussion incident to national preparedness should overshadow the vocational-education bill, but fortunately Congress saw that vocational education and national preparedness were linked together, and the bill passed almost unanimously.

The full significance of the Smith-Hughes Bill, as it will always be known by those who worked for it, can hardly be appreciated. On the surface it merely creates a Federal Board of Vocational Education and provides that federal grants shall be made for the purpose of coöperating with the states in the promotion of industrial, agricultural, and home-making teaching. But if we scratch the surface we shall see that the federal money is not paid to local communities except after their work has been approved by a state board of control on the basis of this federal act, and the principles and policies which were adopted after conference between the Federal Board and the state boards of control. It furthermore limits federal aid to definite vocational training and eliminates all aid to any dilettante or superficial types of practical-arts education which do not meet the idea of preparing young persons over 14 years of age for useful and profitable employment in agriculture, in the trades, in industries, or in home economics. It has been stated in preceding chapters, and will be emphasized more than once in succeeding chapters, that the schools which are able to serve most effectively in time of war are the schools which are serving or may serve in times of peace. It has been and will again be shown that school methods usable in meeting a war emergency are the methods not only usable but desirable under normal conditions.

There is absolutely nothing in the following discussion of the field for war service for industrial and trade-school education which does not have its direct application in promoting and administering a national system of vocational education. Definite suggestions are given for organizing day-industrial, trade, part-time and continuation schools, evening vocational schools, trade classes, and off-time courses; for transferring the teaching equipment into the factory; for transferring the technical-supervision equipment of the factory to the school; and for making commercial products. It will be seen that the service of our industrial and trade schools differs from the service of the industrial and household-arts courses in the regular schools. A comparison of what is suggested for war service with what is required by the terms of the federal grant shows that the two are in accord. For example, the latter requires that all-day industrial schools must have at least half the time given over to the actual practice of a vocation on a useful or productive basis; that agricultural schools shall arrange for directed or supervised practice in agriculture either on a farm provided by the school or on other farms for at least six months a year; that part-time schools or classes must be established if the state and the community expect to receive the full benefits of the federal grant for the salaries of teachers of the trade, home-economics, and industrial subjects; and finally, that evening classes for industrial workers are provided in which the instruction is required to be supplemental to the daily employment. However, for the duration of the war, at least, the last requirement needs modification.

War preparedness undoubtedly influenced Congress to pass the Smith-Hughes Bill. War service of our vocational schools will undoubtedly influence the vocational-education movement along right lines more than anything else which could possibly have happened.

Industrial and trade schools stand ready to make their contribution for war service. Some rather unwisely, and certainly unthinkingly, sent telegrams to Washington, offering their equipment to the government. Others said that they would make ammunition. Still others announced that they would wait for the government to tell them what to do. In the early stages evidently most of them forgot that their chief, if not only, business must be, as it has been, that of training recruits for industry or giving trade extension work to those already in a chosen vocation.

Of course we are all aware that new tasks of stupendous proportions are being undertaken by the country as measures for national defense, and that while a large army is being recruited and trained, a still larger army is being drawn into industrial production to equip and support the army and navy directly on the lines of defense. We know that $600,000,000 has been appropriated for aëroplane construction; that from 50,000 to 100,000 shipbuilders are needed for our shipbuilding program; that tool-makers and gauge-makers are needed in large numbers; that the government military service will require large numbers of mechanics in its quartermaster's, engineering, signal, aviation, and navy corps.

In other words, there is convincing evidence that there are bound to be not only increased demands for labor but also changes in the relationship of labor demand and supply. There is going to be an enormous increase in the demand for specialist workers in metal, and considerable increase in the call for skilled all-round workers in metal; a material increase in the demand for woodworkers in shipyards; an increase in demand for workers in manufactured clothing and army equipment; a great increase in demand for electrical workers in all lines, including operators, field men, telephone and telegraph service. We know that there will be a demand for automobile mechanics, gas-engine operators, plumbers, horseshoers, wheelwrights, steam engineers, bakers, cement workers, and gas and steam fitters. It is probable that there will be a diminution in the demand for printers; for women in dressmaking, millinery, and novelty lines; for laborers on public works, including streets, sewers, water systems, public buildings, canals, and bridges.

In short, we know that the war emergency will create an extraordinary demand for some kinds of labor, attended by a probable diminution of demand for other kinds, and there will be occasion for much shifting of labor from one occupation to another. It is obvious, furthermore, that many readjustments must be made by public and private industrial and trade schools in these days of war pressure.

To determine what adjustments are most urgent, those in charge of these schools should go directly to the industries and confer as to what service is the most desired. It is practically useless to wait for industrial managers to come to the schools for help. In many cases they will not appreciate the fact that the schools can be of help. If, in times of peace, industry has hardly recognized the full possibilities of public vocational training, it is not likely that it would recognize it in the stress of increased production. Sir Robert Blair of London states that unless the educational staff of England had made it its business to satisfy the manufacturers that it could train semiskilled workers, the vocational-training shops would have been obliged to close soon after the war started. He states that in the earliest days of the work of these training shops, the manufacturers were indisposed to believe that industry had anything to learn from trade or technical schools. The manufacturers said that these schools were "academically right and practically wrong."

What industrial and trade schools can do for manufacturing plants will, of course, vary in each community. Each manufacturing center has its own sets of activities. Proper military authorities should be approached by administrators of industrial schools to determine what can be contributed toward providing the training which is needed. Letters to military authorities in Washington will not bear so much fruit as a personal visit to a local recruiting station, camp, or cantonment for definite advice as to how schools may best serve. It is expected, however, that the National Board of Vocational Education will be helpful with suggestive material.

At the present moment the most effective contact between the school that may give the training and the place that needs it can be brought about through coöperation either with cantonment authorities or with local manufacturing plants. Industrial and technical schools in England in the early days of the war formed connections with government arsenals and began the manufacture of gauges for shell-making, mostly of the inspection type. At first the technical institutes were very diffident about undertaking the work, the standard of skill required being so high; but after a few appeals on the ground that it was a great opportunity for trade education to show its value, the institutions started the work, so that there are now something like a dozen such schools working on the manufacture of these instruments. It is to be understood that the majority of the workers thus employed were metal workers before they took up this work. Others were manual-training teachers in the elementary schools. They have turned out approximately 50,000 inspection gauges, and it is the opinion in England that the trade institutes never undertook a better work.

In general terms the shortage of help in the industries is going to be met by training operatives selected from unskilled workers; by training foremen of those operatives who will be selected from the skilled help; and by training highly skilled specialists who will be selected from the workmen already skilled. The training plan in the New England Westinghouse plant will be interesting in this connection. In this ammunition plant 80 per cent of the workers are listed as operators, the majority of whom are trained from carefully selected unskilled labor. To train these operators skilled machinists are employed as instructors. One instructor is in charge of a group averaging about thirteen men. In other words, $7\frac{1}{2}$ per cent of the force in the operating departments are on the instruction staff and known as foremen, linemen (set-up men), and instructors. Instruction is given incidentally in turning out the regular product. No equipment is set aside primarily for instruction purposes; any equipment in the plant may be thus used. This method of instruction is called the group-instructor plan, in which one instructor or foreman has charge of teaching a group of operators working on an assigned task. While under instruction the group is employed on regular production. The instructor is not required to produce, but gives his entire time to group teaching. In the tool-making department, men of mechanical ability, not necessarily all-round machinists, but in some instances from other trades, are trained in making jigs and fixtures. In these cases the ratio of instructors to workers is less than one to thirteen, the helper plan being used. The helper plan is that in which a skilled worker is employed in special work, such as tool-making or gauge-making, and has under him from one to three helpers. In this case the man who gives the training does not confine his entire efforts to instruction, but is required to work at his particular occupation. If satisfactory results are to be secured, only a very limited number of helpers can be assigned to one worker.

The industrial schools will prove to be a small factor in training operatives, in view of the fact that industry itself is able to train them quickly and satisfactorily. It takes only a few days to make a Polish farm hand of Connecticut into an ammunition worker in Bridgeport. Foremen and specialists may be trained through evening and day part-time courses. Of course it is assumed that these schools will have equipment requisite for training in the kind of work for which help is needed. The Springfield (Massachusetts) Vocational School expects to shift some of its pupils from house to ship carpentry in view of the new demand for men with a knowledge of shipbuilding, — a demand which will extend, undoubtedly, over a term of years.

At least, one way for a trade school to be of service and yet not purchase additional equipment is to lend its skilled instructors to a local manufacturing plant where an organized plan for training foremen and specialists exists. This has been done by the Quincy (Massachusetts) Industrial School, which coöperates in furnishing part of the instruction given in the Fore River shipbuilding plant.

This company is giving instruction to a selected group of workers under pay for a full industrial day of ten hours. A night shift of training for eleven hours is also given to another group of men. Instructors are training an assigned group of operators on regular production and under usual employment conditions. Some part-time instruction in technical subjects, and in some cases on special operations, is also given to certain groups of selected workers while under employment in the plant. This plan has a significance worthy of attention after the war.

General Manager Smith of this company, at a conference of state administrators of vocational schools held the middle of July in New York City, made an interesting statement as to the need of trained help in the shipyards. A summary of his remarks follows: [1]

For shipbuilding purposes men trained in the building trades offer little advantage over intelligent untrained men, as the character of work in the shipbuilding industry is so different from that in the building trades.

However, industrial and trade schools can give preliminary and thorough instruction to ship-fitters and loftsmen. The course for the latter should include ship-drafting.

[1] Taken from bulletin of the National Society for the Promotion of Industrial Education, for August, 1917, " War Demands for Industrial Training."

More limited instruction can be given in other ironworkers' trades and in the shipwright trades.

Trained instructors are needed. Instructors may be employed in the plant and, if so, should have full power to instruct and should not be employed on production, as the best results in instruction can only be obtained by having the instructor concentrate his mind on his work.

Shipbuilding in the United States has been one of our smaller industries. If the present crisis is to be adequately met, the industry will be one of our most important ones.

Of the large amount of money to be spent in shipbuilding, practically one half will be expended on labor in the shipyard; the remainder is for material purchased from outside parties, but which at the works of such subcontractors is again largely labor. Of the labor expended in the shipyard about one third is for ironworkers, and it is in this trade that the greatest shortage occurs, as there is only a small percentage of men for the ironworkers' trade now to be found in this country.

In the past very little instruction in the specialized shipbuilding trades has been given in the United States, and the number of men who have served apprenticeship in these trades is small, a great supply of skilled men in these trades coming from Great Britain. There is an imperative need for a supply of men in the ironworkers' trade.

Some instruction must always be given in the shipbuilding plant, but it is possible to give a great deal in the industrial schools, and, as the wages are good, men should be readily attracted to the shipbuilding trades.

While ironworkers' trades consisting of loftsmen, shipfitters, riveters, chippers, calkers, reamers, bolters, packers, and some others are peculiar to shipbuilding as well as the shipwright's trade, the trades of plumber, pipe fitter, coppersmith, etc. are very materially different in the shipbuilding trades from what they are in the building trades.

On the other hand, it is possible to send instructors from the factories to the school. In several instances in England the manufacturers supplied the schools with instructors and all the necessary material in order to teach women and boys the identical operations which they would be called upon to carry out in the factory. In this way a number of schools combining manufacturing with training were able to supply local factories with boys and women trained in the special operations involved. This plan is also significant and has an important bearing upon the administration of public vocational training.

The question whether industrial schools should make ammunition or equipment pertaining to war service will come up. Having substantial amounts of available equipment, they will doubtless at times be tempted to use their organized day and evening classes for purposes of emergency productive work. In machine-shop schools, for example, the teachers being skilled machinists and the pupils capable of turning out a substantial amount of productive work, inducements to subordinate educational ends to those of an economic nature may be expected. It is therefore suggested that industrial-school authorities resolutely resist all attempts to subordinate their rightful purpose of giving industrial education. It is clear that a certain amount of production is necessary for purposes of education, but it is important that this should never be made a primary purpose in any industrial school. A letter from Director W. C. Smith of the Troy (New York) Central School illustrates the productive work of one school which retains educational value.

A Troy corporation is engaged on a large contract with the government for uniforms. Its shops are taxed to the limit, and it has found it necessary to utilize every available shop in town for making various machines used in cutting cloth for this contract. It has entered into an arrangement whereby our complete machine-shop equipment is turned over to its use under the supervision of our own instructor. Our graduate boys are employed in the shop and are now at work perfecting twelve machines for use in different parts of the country on this contract.

The public vocational schools must face, sooner or later, the question of shop production on a commercial basis. They exist, primarily, to train producers and not to make products. Are the two inconsistent? Perhaps the war service of these schools will bring this debatable issue to a head.

Obviously the industries engaged in the making of automobiles, aëroplanes, machinery, and ammunition have for some time past absorbed the available supply of skilled help. With the emergency of war preparation upon us, we must find ways of pressing thousands of workers into lines of work with which they are almost altogether unfamiliar. Except with boys who are fourteen to sixteen years old, it will be of little avail to think of giving all-round trade training. The labor supply which we now need must be trained immediately and intensively. From what has already been stated it is clear that workers may be trained in three ways: first, in day industrial or technical schools; second, in industrial plants such as have been mentioned in the case of the Westinghouse Company; third, through part-time employment in industry, with part-time attendance in industrial or technical schools.

The industrial-school authorities should send into the factories capable instructors who have had trade experience, in order to learn the needs for trained help and to analyze the trade processes for which men need to be trained. In this way the school may determine whether it can best meet the situation by training the youth in its day schools to go to work in industrial plants upon leaving school — although this is not a very immediate way of meeting the emergency — or whether it would be better to move the classes, so to speak, over to the plant and have the instructors teach a group of unskilled workers on the group-instruction plan. Perhaps the school could perform its best service by giving trade extension courses to those already engaged in productive work. Anyhow, these alternatives must be fully considered.

These instructors or trained experts, when visiting typical yards or plants in a specific industry to learn of the needs for trained help, must be able to reanalyze the trade processes in terms of training as distinct from terms of production, and out of this analysis to draw up suitable schemes for giving such training. The question of whether this training should be given entirely in the school or entirely in the plant or partly in the plant and partly in the school should be left to experts, who know best the possibilities of each of these schemes.

This is no time for industrial schools to stand on their dignity and claim that they can do all that is necessary in their day schools without coöperation with those who employ. It is readily granted that, generally speaking, directors of industrial schools know their job quite well when it comes to giving trade-preparatory training to youth before it enters industry; but at a time when the country needs thousands of workmen we are quite sure that the better plan for training operators and semiskilled workers is directly in the plant itself. In a time of great emergency this intensive, immediate training must be given in large part by the industries themselves within their own plants. They have the equipment, they have the men who need the training; all they lack is the proper instructing force, as they cannot take men away from production for instruction purposes. It follows that the instructors of our schools must give their instruction in the plants or must have the unskilled operatives and helpers come to the school for part-time work.

The present all-day industrial schools, even in normal times, need this direct contact with industry to save themselves from shop methods which savor of manual-training schools.

It is assumed that the regular all-day industrial and trade schools will continue. Of course they are now largely attended by comparatively young students, and it is quite likely that the enrollment will diminish, as there is an unusual demand for boys in every branch of industry and commerce. It will be increasingly difficult to hold such boys in school in the face of financial returns rather extraordinary when one considers their youth.

In the interests of conservation of youth and the training of a suitable supply of skilled workers for the future, there should be no diminution of effort to develop and extend day-school work, even though the young people thus trained will be too young to contribute definitely to the present emergency, unless, of course, it should last more than a year or two. Nevertheless, the enrollments are likely to be less. A partial compensation for this situation is that groups of more mature workers coming from the industry itself on a part-time basis can be accommodated for special instruction, or groups of young men who are now elevator boys, messenger boys, clerks in stores, office boys, can be induced, perhaps, to come to the all-day school, and through short, intensive courses be put into the way of earning, in some factory making war supplies, a sum equal to from two to three times what they are now earning. No attempt should be made to hold such youths in the school beyond the period necessary to give them immediate and intensive training.

After the war it will be an open question whether intensive courses should not be more generally adopted in our day industrial schools.

Obviously the largest immediate service that can be rendered by industrial and trade schools will be through the readjustment and extension of evening and other off-time courses. As usual, the especially important function will be the training of men already in the trades for more skilled tasks or for directive work. Ways must be found for extending the evening-school facilities. One way is to operate the evening courses throughout the entire year. Most of our industrial schools operate only from October to April, but in this time of pressure they should be open continuously. The other way would be to carry on trade extension work not only in the evening but also early in the morning or late in the afternoon. These are technically known as off-time courses and came into existence originally in some cities which made provision for training workers from plants operating night shifts.

Fundamentally, even in times of peace, there is no sound reason for ever completely closing a day industrial school. It might run during the summer as well as the winter; in the late afternoon and early morning as well as in the evening. In the middle of June, 1917, President Wilson addressed a letter to Secretary Redfield making the suggestion that the vocational-training schools of the country should be open during the summer, when it would be possible to train a large number of young men under military age, either to fill the places in our industries left by men who enlist or are withdrawn for military service, or to carry on special occupations called for by the war, such as inspectors of material and apparatus. In this connection, where the President speaks of " inspectors of material," it may be said that one of the prominent industrial-education experts of the East has been asked to train a group of men selected for special government inspection work. These men will then be responsible for organizing a force of assistant inspectors in the plant to which they are assigned, and of supervising the work of the assistant inspector under their personal direction.

The course of inspectorship training is made up of two units: one dealing with the business and accounting side of inspection and the other with the technical instruction which is given through participation in the actual work of inspection at the arsenal, observation of the manufacturing processes, and direct group instruction.

The first unit is given at Washington and usually requires from four or five days to a week for its completion. The second unit is given at the Rock Island arsenal and covers eleven days as a minimum. Only the most experienced men, however, complete it in this length of time. The men enter the school at irregular intervals in groups of four or five at a time. The number in training at any one time varies from thirty-five to fifty.

The men are moved from department to department on a fixed schedule. When a man completes his training he is assigned to a plant in accordance with his qualifications as indicated by his previous experience and his record at the school. Further plans for training the inspector after he has been assigned to the field have been proposed but have not yet been put into effect. Many of the candidates for this training are instructors in vocational training.[1]

The opportunity for promotion of skilled workers was never so great as at present, and the opportunity for schools to train them will never be greater than at present. The schools may well organize intensive short courses in practical training, as well as other courses designed to advance qualified workers to positions of directive work in the factories.

While the part-time plan offers excellent opportunities for advancing selected workers in order that they may acquire certain technical knowledge, it is doubtful whether much of this work during this emergency period can be done in the public or private industrial and trade schools. We all know that certain industrial concerns have established part-time schools in their plants. These classes in the works are especially adapted, in the present emergency, for training selected workers to become specialists and foremen. If the school is near

[1] "Vocational Education and Government Service," News-letter issued by National Society for the Promotion of Industrial Education, October, 1917.

War needs open new fields for schools. After the war, stereotyped courses in trade schools and technical institutes will have lost their hold. Dunwoody Institute (Minneapolis, Minnesota) is one of the few schools having a training course for bakers

An example of an effective adaptation to a national need. Dunwoody Institute meeting a shortage of army bakers

Educational efficiency as measured by its response to a national need. Dunwoody Institute is one of the several institutes teaching radiography and power testing to navy men

the plant, so that industrial workers can attend for part-time day instruction for a period of six or eight hours a week without loss of time or without interfering with production, it may be possible to develop some part-time courses in the schools, but, generally speaking, it would be better for the instructors in these schools to go directly to the plants themselves and give this part-time instruction there. In another chapter mention will be made of a feasible part-time system and the necessity for some such system, but it refers only to boys and girls between fourteen and sixteen years old who belong primarily in school and not primarily at work. It is assumed that the group of which we have been thinking is the older group of workmen who wish to become foremen.

Sir Robert Blair, in his report already referred to, speaks of the manner in which technical and trade schools in and about London train semi-skilled workers for munition work.

At first we gathered together all the metal-working apparatus of our elementary schools and placed it in two of our technical institutes. Shafting was put up, power was installed and the lathes started, and they have been running ever since July, 1915, for twelve hours a day in three periods of four hours each. At first the period of training was for one period a day for six days a week for six weeks, or a total of 144 hours, but later, to meet the demands, the manufacturers took upon themselves the training of more highly skilled turners, of machine erectors, of milling-machine hands, and so on. We began to train women for tracing in drawing offices and subsequently for mechanical drawing. We trained lead-burners for employment in factories making explosives. We trained gauge-makers for employment in tool rooms of our shell factories (many of these men have been drawn from the jewelry and silversmithing trades). The more skill we gave the training, the longer it took to train these people, and so the number produced weekly has diminished, but in two years we have trained, certified, and placed 6000 workers.

And again he speaks of other training apart from furnishing additional munition workers.

One institution has done a great deal of work in training in cold shoeing over 1000 men belonging to the Royal Field Artillery, Royal Engineers, and the Army Service Corps. The same institution has also been used for the reception, inspection, and dispatch of many of the horse-shoes required by the army. At another institution over 3500 students have been trained for Red Cross duties, and a great work has been done in recruiting men for the skilled sections of the Royal Flying Corps. Besides we have trained men for tinsmithing, copper work, and wireless telegraphy. A third institution took on the general direction of the preparation of synthetic drugs in the chemical departments of the technical institutes, and the medical organization of the army was largely indebted to these chemical departments for the production of the much-needed drugs.

Assuming that administrators of industrial education are interested in the welfare of factory workers, — something often apart from instilling technical skill and knowledge, — it will be necessary for them to provide courses for men and especially for women workers, giving instruction in the laws of health with which every employee in factory life should be familiar. In England the memoranda of the British Health of Munition Workers Committee have demonstrated conclusively the great necessity of this teaching of hygiene: that the causes of ill health of workers in munitions factories were not alone the result of fatigue from long hours, but quite as much the result of insufficient or ill-prepared food, inadequate sleep and ill-ventilated sleeping quarters, and failure to appreciate the consequences of disregarding safety devices.

It may not be amiss in this chapter to say a word about our government naval schools, for some may not be aware that the government has for a number of years been maintaining a very efficient system of trade education. The purpose of the naval trade schools is to train young men for various trades or occupations required on shipboard. In going over the list it is likely that administrators of industrial education will see an opportunity to connect the work of their schools with the work of the naval schools. In addition to the practical instruction given at the training stations where these schools are located, a course of academic instruction is conducted throughout the naval service. This instruction does not stop at the training station, but continues on shipboard, and every encouragement is given for advancement. Electrical schools are located at the Brooklyn Navy Yard and at Mare Island, California. The course of instruction comprises machine-shop work, reciprocating steam engines, steam-turbine engines, internal-combustion engines, magnetism and electricity, dynamos, motors, motor generators, alternating-current batteries, etc. Members of the radio class are trained in the duties of a radio operator and are given constant practice in the use of the mechanism employed in recovering and sending messages.

The artificer school is located at the Norfolk Navy Yard, and is composed of classes for ship-wrights, ship-fitters, blacksmiths, and painters.

The machinist and coppersmith schools are located at Charleston, South Carolina, and are open only to reënlisted men who have certain experience.

The aëronautics school is located at Pensacola, Florida, and is divided into two courses: mechanics of aëronautics, and flying.

Gasoline-engine instruction is given at Charlestown Navy Yard in connection with the machinist's school, preference being given to reënlisted men.

Commissary schools for ships' cooks, bakers, and stewards are located at San Francisco and Newport.

Musicians' schools are maintained at Norfolk, at Great Lake, Illinois, and at San Francisco.

Seaman-gunner schools are located at the Washington Navy Yard and at the torpedo station at Newport.

All of these schools give short, intensive courses ranging from three to eighteen months in length. The students are paid wages, and all expenses are met the same as with other enlisted men.

Seven free marine-engineering schools and thirty free navigation schools are being started on the Atlantic, Gulf, Pacific, and Great Lakes coasts to train men already having some experience for better places at advanced pay as engineers and deck officers in the new merchant fleet. The graduates are being placed as fast as they are graduated. The need for their services is expected to last for many years after peace is restored.

For several years our industrial continuation schools have had as their motto " Earn and Learn." But the naval technical schools have shown a way whereby young men may both serve and learn.

CHAPTER IV

OUR COLLEGES AND TECHNICAL INSTITUTES

It is to be hoped that if we can realize, as England did not, that education, to quote Arnold Bennett, "is the very last thing that we ought to economize in," we shall spare ourselves some of the unnecessary calamities of war. England, France, Italy, and the Central Powers have thrown into battle a very large percentage of their educated and trained men, including most of the young professors and instructors in their universities and colleges, gymnasiums, and *lycées*. Their colleges and universities are almost empty. The young men who would under normal conditions be receiving the education and training necessary to prepare them for leadership in the future development of these countries are fighting and dying in the trenches.

In view of the fact that all of these countries must needs go through a long period of reconstruction, industrial and otherwise, it is a pity that the sacrifice of its best youth had needlessly to be made. As a matter of fact, we see now that no university, college, or technical school that can possibly avoid it should permit its faculty or student body to be scattered or its energies dissipated. All concerned should redouble their energies and concentrate them upon those things which will be of the most service in the progress of the war and will prepare the students for the most effective service when the war is over.

President Wilson, three months after the severing of relations with Germany, in response to a request for an opinion on the continuance of a college or a technical-school education during the war, wrote this letter:

The question which you have brought to my attention is of the very greatest moment. It would, as you suggest, seriously impair American prospects of success in this war if the supply of highly trained men were unnecessarily diminished. There will be need for a larger number of persons expert in the various fields of applied science than ever before. Such persons will be needed both during the war and after its close.

I have therefore no hesitation in urging colleges and technical schools to endeavor to maintain their courses as far as possible on the usual basis. There will be many young men from these institutions who will serve in the armed forces of the country. Those who fall below the age of selective conscription and who do not enlist may feel that by pursuing their courses with earnestness and diligence they also are preparing themselves for valuable service to the nation.

I would particularly urge upon the young people who are leaving our high schools that as many of them as can do so avail themselves this year of the opportunities offered by the colleges and technical schools, to the end that the country may not lack an adequate supply of trained men and women.

It must be said that while students were restless and anxious to perform a service, the college authorities themselves adopted a very hopeless and helpless attitude toward the war in so far as it reacted on the internal economy of these institutions. Commencement exercises were abbreviated and shorn of their customary festivities. College presidents and executive committees of alumni associations began to "talk poor" and to wax lugubrious over the small senior class of 1918. These men even wanted to drop athletics, which, to the facetious layman outside, constitutes the main reason for a college's existence. The general action of the colleges in this matter of abandoning so many athletic and other activities drew from President Wilson a letter deprecating such action and advising that the colleges maintain all their usual sports if they did not detract in any way from the military purpose of the nation. In an address at Princeton University, Major General Wood deplored hasty action of students in enlisting for service in the army and navy, urging them to complete their school work for the year, and that they mark time pending the carrying out of provisions of the selective-draft law.

It is clear, on one hand, that many college authorities, especially those of the older type, passed through a state of academic institutional hysteria, while, on the other hand, their student bodies translated the emotions of the moment into a deep conviction by enlisting.

At the same time the spirit of mobilization was present in many a university, college, and technical school. In the cultural college it was the individual who enlisted, as the institution was not of the type whose work directly and definitely counted for important war service. In the universities where courses are given in agriculture, in medicine, in technology, and in practical arts, the institution itself enlisted, in that it offered war-emergency courses.

It is perhaps interesting at this point to see how response came from these two types of institutions. In the first instance it came from individuals in the college, which was no more than could be expected of classical colleges, which have for years laid emphasis on the benefits of individualistic training. In the second instance the vocational colleges, as they are sometimes disparagingly called, responded from the viewpoint of collectivism; that is, the

college as a whole, because of its service departments, was able to offer to the state and to the
nation a course of training of immediate military
value to the country.

But thoughtful people can never again speak
disparagingly of any university or technical school.
While the movies have been filled with the citizens of our democracy, and the cafés crowded with
people to whom war was something apart from
existence, and the white-light gayety of the streets
has been apparently undimmed, the youth of our
colleges — the best youth in the world — have enlisted in Plattsburgs, joined the Naval Reserves,
taken up signal-corps work, entered the research
laboratory, followed their instructors into the medical corps, joined a school of aëronautics, or donned
overalls in the shipyards.

Doctor Finley, Commissioner of Education of
the state of New York, in an address delivered
before the Illinois chapter of the Phi Beta Kappa,
speaks of his visit to Oxford just before the war
and of a visit to Cambridge, England, a few weeks
after it had begun. At Oxford he found the calm
of the cloister, with its memorials of poets, scholars,
statesmen, princes, and soldiers, where there were
ancient academic conventions that paid no heed
to the passing customs of the world outside. Only

six weeks later at Cambridge — a Cambridge which had a month or six weeks before been as Oxford — the town was filled with men in khaki. In this charming address Doctor Finley speaks of a portrait of Samuel Butler which he saw at Cambridge, — a portrait of the man who described in his book " Erewhon " a land where criminals were treated as sick, and the sick as criminals; where there were " Colleges of Unreason," colleges in which students were promoted for excellence in vagueness and were plucked for insufficient trust in printed matter, colleges where the principal courses were those in hypothetics, colleges in which mediocrity was fostered, colleges whose graduates almost invariably suffered from atrophy of individual opinions. And Doctor Finley says that as he stood before this portrait, in a hall almost deserted, he thought of those students of courses which Butler had called "hypothetical" and " atrophying," who had gone forth to prove the valor of their cloistered and unpractical learning.

The university which apparently had paid no heed to the passing customs of the world outside had now mobilized herself; and this has been true of the colleges and technical schools of our own country, — truly a mobilization of the spirit of sudden forgetting of self-concerns for a selfless service.

The college of individualism, as has already been suggested, mobilized through its individuals, while the college of service mobilized itself. In the spring of 1917 I happened to be in a Western university. The campus was practically deserted. Instructors in foreign languages had joined the government interpreters' service; some of the professors of science had gone to government research laboratories, while a chosen few were off in some secret place working under government direction in scientific research concerning submarine warfare. The older students had enlisted, and the younger ones were marching in squads on the athletic field. Truly a mobilization, but largely individualistic.

I came East to another college where more than 2000 students were devoting their time to a series of special short courses dealing with the various problems of an educational, social, and practical nature which the war had thrust upon the country. In this way the institution — Teachers College, Columbia University — had mobilized itself. Special arrangements had been made by the college authorities whereby all but a very few students could participate in these emergency courses without seriously deranging their regular courses.

In general, the aim of these emergency courses

was not merely to meet those conditions which exist at or near the battle line but to help in the solution of the hundred and one urgent problems which must be solved by that great majority of teachers and social workers whose service will of necessity be given in home communities. Accordingly, courses on social relief were offered, and among others the following topics were considered: " Administration of relief in time of war and emergency," " Care of orphaned and neglected children." Under the organization of rural communities were discussed " Conserving the food supply," " The health problem of the rural community," and " The organization of school pupils for agricultural service." The matter of social service in military camps was thoroughly gone into and reports and lectures were given by men who had actually worked with the soldiers themselves. The Boy Scout and Camp Fire Girl movements were also discussed in special courses, and the practical questions of the amateur gardener were carefully considered.

In the School of Practical Arts special attention was given to the making of children's garments, the sewing of Red Cross material, and the renovating of millinery and clothing. In addition to lectures on thrift in food the department of cookery gave a course on emergency cookery for men,

which was especially designed for army cooks and
Boy Scout leaders. There was also a series of lectures and demonstrations by a government expert
on the preservation of food, including canning and
drying. Other courses considered the essentials of
diet planning and of how to buy in large quantities
for camps and hospitals. The departments of chemistry and biology gave special instruction in the
analysis of water and of milk, and in the technique of diagnostic bacteriology. The fine-arts
department made some rather unique contributions, including a study of protective coloring with
reference to *camouflage* for military purposes, the
designing of posters, and topographical sketching.
There was a course on tin-can work for home
and camp, in which, from discarded tomato cans
and powder boxes, were produced all sorts of
useful things — coffee pots, camp stoves, hot-water
bottles, lanterns, and candlesticks. A special course
in photography for hospital and field work was
offered. In the modeling class the manipulation of
plaster of Paris was demonstrated for nurses and
Red Cross students, to be used in connection with
occupational work for convalescent soldiers. An
extremely interesting series of projects in plastic
material was worked up, particularly some clay
models of trenches and dugouts.

Another course which attracted some hundred and fifty students was the emergency instruction given by the physics department in automobile mechanics. The object of the instruction was to equip the average student with a stock of general information that would enable him to operate a car, to make minor repairs, and to diagnose trouble intelligently. Some of the matters discussed were the four-cycle engine, carburetion, transmission and differential, and the storage battery. For experiment and demonstration purposes the laboratory was supplied, among other apparatus, with a detachable boat motor and two automobiles. The latter were thoroughly dissected and then reassembled from spark plug to tires, and in every possible way the mechanism was examined and experimented with.

The departments of nursing and health and of physical education offered some ten courses in all, including home nursing and emergencies, surgical dressings, care of children, public-health problems, first aid, medical gymnastics, and invalid occupations.

The department of music offered three courses designed especially to prepare students to lead music appropriate to patriotic meetings and to present selections at hospitals and camps.

Two courses were offered by the department of speech: one planned for those intending to do emergency speaking and lecturing, and the other arranged to meet the demand for entertainment for little children, the sick, and soldiers during the war.

In addition to these technical courses there was a series of lectures on economic problems contributed by various Columbia experts, and another series of special lectures by such speakers as Mr. Joseph McCabe, the noted English author, and Mr. Frederick C. Wolcott, director of the Polish War Relief Commission. Finally, there was a wonderful and never-to-be-forgotten address by Ignace Paderewski, in which he reviewed the long and troubled story of his native land and in impassioned words pleaded for the restoration of Poland's ancient liberties.

It may be said without exaggeration that in all some millions of people throughout the United States will, directly and indirectly, profit by this emergency instruction at Teachers College, for the students who attended are for the most part experienced teachers, who, in their turn, will organize and instruct their home communities in similar preparedness courses.

At the same time another university, unique in

its way, — the University of the State of New York, — was holding, through its Board of Regents, a meeting to determine academic standards of the schools and colleges of the state in a war crisis. This university was modeled upon the University of France, the constituent units of which have proved themselves wonderful instruments in the waging of war. The universities represented have organized themselves into a civil army, preventing the wastes of duplication, misdirected endeavor, and isolation so common everywhere.

In the building where the Board of Regents met, two conferences were being held, one representing the schools and colleges of the state, the other representing the agricultural and industrial interests. In one place men were discussing how the academic status of professional schools and colleges might be maintained, and in another room men and women were participating in a discussion of public markets, food conservation, services of agricultural teachers, the taking of an agricultural census, the releasing of boys from school, the organizing of canning clubs, and all those affairs of the state and its schools which might contribute to the nation's welfare. These two meetings offered a picture of two lines of work which must always go together in time of war.

As Commissioner Claxton has said:

Students should be made to understand that it is their duty to give to their country and to the world the best and fullest possible measure of service, for both country and world will need more than they will get of that high type of service which only men and women of the best education and training can give. Patriotism and desire to serve humanity may require of these young men and women the exercise of that very high type of self-restraint which will keep them to their tasks of preparation until the time comes when they can render service which cannot be rendered by others.

On the other hand, these same colleges and schools must contribute out of themselves that important vocational service so necessary in time of war, and the gathering at this meeting of agricultural and household-arts teachers, of farm-bureau men and county agents, of representatives from granges and women's clubs, of bankers, and of publicists was after all typical of the other half of the university or school contribution.

At this meeting of the Regents the following resolutions were adopted on the recommendation of the administrators of schools and colleges who were in conference with the Regents. These resolutions are given in full because they express significantly the point of view of the 36 colleges and 964 secondary schools in New York State.

1. Realizing that one of the most urgent needs of the country in the present crisis will be the training of officers for military service, and that it is the peculiar duty of colleges and universities to contribute in supplying this need, we recommend that the several colleges and universities in the state establish one or more units of the Reserve Officers Training Corps, as provided in general order No. 49, including courses leading at the same time to a commission and to a college degree.

2. In order that the extraordinary burdens and sacrifices of war may be shared in just proportion by all the nation, and that the calamitous experiences of the past under the voluntary system may be avoided, it is our judgment that in the raising of the necessary military forces the principle of universal obligation to service be applied by a process of selective conscription.

3. That members in good standing of the graduating classes of the professional schools of the state who shall have been accepted for military service by the government be granted their degrees without special examination.

4. That members in good standing of the graduating classes in the undergraduate departments of the colleges and universities of the state who would normally be graduated in June, 1917, and who shall be accepted for military service by the government should be granted their degrees without special examination.

5. That members of the graduating classes in the high schools of the state who would normally be graduated in June, 1917, and who have been accepted for military service shall be granted their diplomas, and that the colleges of the state be requested to honor these diplomas for purposes of admission.

6. That college students in good standing pursuing medical preparatory courses who enlist or are called into military service before the completion of the college year be granted certificates of completion of their year without examination.

7. That absence from college or high school by reason of enlistment in military service shall not prejudice the award or the retention of university scholarships.

8. That while the immediate service which women may perform in connection with the war will be in medicine or nursing and other work for general public welfare, and that while the greatest service for which they may eventually be called will be the supplying of positions vacated by the enlisted men, we recommend to the United States government the appointment by the Council for National Defense of a commission which shall outline an appropriate policy for women students in our colleges, with respect both to their college studies and to their enlistment for national service.

9. That this board approve the plans of the National Research Council and proffer our hearty coöperation.

10. That students in colleges and universities of the state who are liable for military training under the military-training law be exempt from the training prescribed by the Military Training Commission if they pursue courses in military training under approved instruction at their respective institutions.

Further, that as there are numerous resources in both the elementary and the secondary schools of the state which can be used to advantage at this time, — among the most important of which resources are the use of high-school pupils for the farms and for necessary clerical and other work that can be done by pupils who remain in school, the use of teachers for summer work, the services possible through industrial and household-arts departments, and the enlistment of upper-grade children for home gardens, — the board adopts the following resolutions :

1. That the State Agricultural Department in conjunction with the State Education Department formulate a plan for enlisting and placing high-school boys upon the farms, for directing and supervising the work of such boys, for determining qualifications as to age and fitness, for determining compensation and school credit, and for the adjustment of any other problems connected with the safeguarding of these boys who enlist for farm service.

2. That the State Education Department secure through the necessary sources a statement of the needs that might be met through the industrial and household-arts departments and other resources of the schools herein stated, and transmit such a statement to the schools of the state, to the end that these resources may be used intelligently and through regularly constituted channels.

3. That the State Education Department consider the practicability of securing some provision by which during the summer vacation and at other times of the year boys 12 years of age or over may be employed if a certificate of proper working conditions can be furnished.

It is impracticable to outline even briefly all that the various colleges and institutes have contributed to war service. The Massachusetts Institute of Technology is hardly mentioned in what follows, and yet it is conducting a score of activities of immediate emergency value. Drexel Institute has contributed not only courses but also its president, Doctor Godfrey, who is serving as a member of the National Council of Defense in special charge of war needs as met by education and science.

To name all the institutions which are serving in one way or another is to call the roll of nearly every college and technical institution in the country. To give here a brief account of what a few are doing will show the range of the activities and the nature of the service.

Early in May Columbia University inaugurated a series of emergency courses of a military, naval, and general nature arranged for the purpose of training students who desire to serve the national government in time of war. They were classified as intensive courses and were opened without restriction to all those who desired to be trained in any of the various subjects offered. These courses included military map making, field-service regulations, general telegraphy, radio telegraphy, camp sanitation, map reading and map interpretation, practical navigation, and electrical devices of the navy.

Harvard University has many achievements to her credit, for example: advanced training for selected officers under the leadership of six French officers;

a cadet school for ensigns; a naval school for wireless operators; a course in orthopedic surgery; the furnishing of the medical personnel for four base hospital units; and war service by departments of dentistry, medicine, psychology, and foreign languages.

Iowa State College gave a six weeks' course in special military and military-engineering work. Regular two-year noncollegiate courses were offered electrical workers and stationary engineers, mechanical draftsmen and mechanics, structural draftsmen and building superintendents, surveyors and road makers.

At Cornell University all professors and instructors in the marine-engineering department and all the senior students of marine engineering were in either private or public shipyards on or before graduation day.

The University of Wisconsin, anticipating that a large number of persons who had been trained in the administration of stores would soon be needed in the civil section of the Quartermaster's Department, in the Ordnance Bureau of the War Department, and in the Quartermaster's Officers' Reserve Corps, decided to aid in training for these services by offering special courses in the classification and handling of stores for those departments.

This university also planned a summer session with courses in wireless telegraphy, first aid to the injured, Boy Scout movement in theory and practice, and gave a course of war lectures especially designed for teachers, and a course for Red Cross volunteers who wished to take part in civilian relief work. This last course was in coöperation with the Red Cross organization, which, as explained in another chapter, will have much to do with relieving families deprived of their natural heads. The men and women in this course studied the basis of family life, psychological and economic principles underlying bodily health, the resources of the state to preserve the family group, and methods of social service and friendly visiting.

Aviation schools for training candidates for the aviation corps were established at the University of California, Cornell University, Georgia Institute of Technology, University of Illinois, Massachusetts Institute of Technology, Ohio State University, Princeton, and the University of Texas. The first navy aëronautic school has also been established recently at the Massachusetts Institute of Technology.

The College of the City of New York offered an emergency war course in bookkeeping and office practice to help fit men and women to fill the positions made necessary by the increased work of the national government, and to train people to take the places of those who responded to the call to arms. It also offered its regular winter courses during the summer in order to speed up the graduation of young men already enrolled in the college who might be drafted.

This college also placed in every armory and military headquarters in Greater New York a teacher of conversational French. This work was very popular and highly successful.

The University of Kentucky offered to women and civilians two special courses in its College of Electrical Engineering: a course in automobile engineering especially designed to teach women how to drive and take care of motor ambulances, and a course in wireless telegraphy.

The Pennsylvania State College offered a six weeks' course in storekeeping under the direction of the Quartermaster's Department.

In Massachusetts, through the extension department of the State Board of Education, lessons were given in conversational French in the armories and encampments. In one armory as many as five instructors were engaged in this service. The vocabulary of the soldier being quite unlike the French dictionary, the military terms and expressions actually used were emphasized. Necessary

French slang and words used commonly for distances, rations, arms and equipment, money, measures, and military orders were dwelt upon. Spoken French for doctors and nurses who are going to the front has been given in coöperation with the Metropolitan Chapter of the American Red Cross.

A six months' course in wireless telegraphy for women was offered at Hunter College, New York City, the course of training being in three divisions: laboratory work, technical work, and the use of code. This course was given with the expectation not that women wireless operators will be placed on ships of war or on transports, but rather that they will be placed in land stations and on coastwise steamers, thus releasing men for more active service. It is understood that on the mechanical side the work is harder for the women, but that on the code work they are much quicker than men.

The field for service of a college is not necessarily limited to extending the usefulness of its vocational departments to meet the war-emergency demands. As has already been noted, the department of French may give courses in conversational French in armories and in cantonments. Sir Robert Blair writes:

We had this plan in England, and as volunteering grew to very considerable dimensions towards the close of 1914 and there were tens of thousands of soldiers grouped within the near neighborhood of London, an arrangement was made with the war-office authorities for the teaching of French.

Courses in mathematics applicable to war needs may be given. The college may send tutors to cantonments to give instruction to undergraduates who have not completed their college work and who would like to receive a college diploma. Colleges can coöperate with the Y.M.C.A., to which has been given the privilege of looking after the recreational features in cantonments. American college boys and others will not be satisfied with formal military training. They will want health talks, entertaining and educational lectures, and instruction as to many things helpful in civil as well as in military life.

There is a large opportunity, in a field as yet hardly touched, for departments of psychology in universities to help in selecting men for different branches of war service and to give vocational guidance to men who leave the service unfitted by war work to reënter their former occupations and perhaps untrained to enter a new service. A staff of psychologists is now at work in each of our cantonments applying intelligence ratings.

There are two distinct uses for the ratings which are given the men as a result of the psychological examinations. One of these uses is military and consists in furnishing a commanding officer with the rating of each man in his command, by which he may, if he chooses, be guided in selecting men for promotion, or for special duties requiring more than average intelligence and mental quickness. The other use is medical and is the thing specifically sought — to find men who are so markedly below the average in intelligence as to demand consideration for discharge or for assignment to simple manual work under careful supervision.

The general method of the test is as follows: The men of each company are divided into 4 groups of 75 to 80 each. Each group is first given a simple literacy test which takes about five minutes and shows only which of the men can read and write. The illiterates are withdrawn at this point to be given examinations for manual skill. All those who can read are then given the "group-intelligence examination."

Those who do not get good ratings are now re-examined in a group to discover whether they are merely slow or are of low-grade intelligence. If any fail to make a satisfactory showing, they are grouped with the illiterates who were separated from the rest of the group after the preliminary examination.

All these — illiterates, and literates who have not done well in the group examination — are given tests for manual skill and ingenuity. These tests are such as putting together dissembled mechanisms, etc. After further individual examination those who receive the poorest rating are likely to be considered for discharge or as suited only for manual work under supervision.

Those who display special mental or manual ability are brought to the notice of their company commanders as men who may be given assignments for superior intelligence or skill.

The aims of the entire psychological examination are to measure native intelligence and ability, not schooling; to disclose what a man can do with his head and hands, not what he has learned from books; and to help the medical officers quickly to discover and sift out the extremely incompetent, and thus prevent the inefficiency and injustice resulting from putting men in places which they are not qualified to fill.

Of course there is a tremendous opportunity for the college to help people understand the causes of war. This has already been referred to in the chapter on " War and Community Uses of our Schools."

Colleges having teacher-training departments will have the opportunity of giving short courses to men and women who will take the places of those who have gone to war. There is also a field for great service in discovering ways and means of improving our public-school systems through lessons drawn from the war.

Every college and university has a large library, and this should be examined with a view to discovering its possible contribution to national defense in war time. Aside from their functions of supplying fresh news and judgments of current events, libraries surely have a vital part in that work of organized research which is behind Germany's scientific and industrial efficiency. Successful research rests as much upon adequate and well-organized book resources as upon laboratories and trained men. The plain and immediate duty of a college situated near a cantonment, or having a portion of its student body enlisted in a camp, would seem to be to build up a military library adequate as a center of military information for those who are studying new methods and instruments of attack and defense. Such a library would be a technical library assisting the large number of specialized schools and fields of training for officers and men in every branch of the service and even in different duties in the same branch. Medical libraries of colleges should be available, with new and important material on military hygiene, medicine, sanitation, and surgery, and this material should be given the widest publicity with reference to its usefulness for the military, medical, and hospital corps.

The college library might well lend to a cantonment a member of its library staff for the development of not only a technical library but also a general reading library for those soldiers who desire only general reading.

The geological department of a college can help in deciding on foundation conditions for army-work constructions, on the location of camp sites with reference to topography, drainage, and water supply, and on the location of trenches with reference to dryness, underdrainage, and rock deposits. Such a department can participate in the study of earth vibrations in connection with heavy artillery discharges for the accurate determination of the distances of enemy batteries. It can also help the government in giving more exact training to young men in the interpretation of geological and topographical maps.

It is obvious that the technical college and the technical institute may render the greatest government service through its faculty and student body. Armour Institute of Chicago has a large number of its graduates and older students in concerns which are producing munition supplies and warships. Many have entered the signal service, and a large class in marine engineering has been specifically organized to prepare men for service with the government.

Wentworth Institute in Boston, under the direction of Principal Arthur L. Williston, has been giving instruction in various branches of military engineering to the First Regiment of Engineers of the Fifth District, U. S. A. This regiment was originally an infantry regiment, but the men voluntarily elected to train themselves to become an engineering regiment. The commissioned officers and non-commissioned officers and all the enlisted men gave three nights a week to the work for several months. In addition some sixty of the men in the regiment voluntarily resigned from business positions in order to devote eight to ten hours a day, six days in the week, to the work. This institute instilled what Mr. Williston calls "mechanical gumption" into the enlisted men through short unit courses in mapping and surveying, topographical sketching, and map reading; gasoline-engine operation, repairing, and maintenance; portable steam-power plant construction and operation; electrical-power plant operation; field telephony;

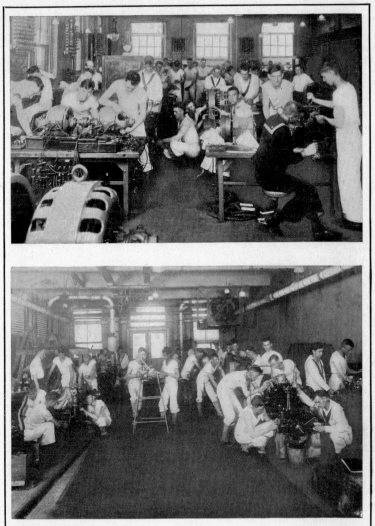

Technical colleges and institutes believe that education is the very last thing in which they ought to economize. Illustrations of class work in national-emergency courses for the army and navy given by Pratt Institute, Brooklyn, New York

A poster which accomplished its purpose. War time, even more than normal times, requires an educational appeal to the work impulses of youth

electric-line construction and maintenance; timber construction, including pontoons, timber trusses, timber suspension-bridge construction, machine-gun shelters, dugouts, and dugout tunneling and framing; strength of materials; concrete construction, including culverts, bridge abutments, gun-carriage and engine foundations; acetylene welding and demolition work; thermite welding and emergency repair; machinery erection and alignment; forging, hardening, and tempering; hydraulics and drainage, especially trench drainage; and rigging. The time was too short to give any elaborate theoretical training. The instruction was given through brief and intensive courses in a very practical way. In many instances it showed men who had practical experience and ability how to adapt their particular kind of skill to the special needs of the given service. Many of these men already had skill, but they needed to have it adapted to military ends.

Pratt Institute, Brooklyn, New York, has been conducting 8 evening classes in machine-shop practice, 6 classes in machine-drafting design, 1 evening class in elementary ship drafting, and day courses for a large body of enlisted men from the navy electrical school and from the signal reserve corps. Those who come from the signal reserve corps are being trained for active service in telegraphy, the institute furnishing the technical instruction in elementary and applied electricity, and army officers furnishing the military and field-service instruction. A mess for the men of this corps is conducted at the school of household science connected with the institute, and here details of men are trained for this work through a course in army cooking. The men from the electrical school are quartered at the navy yard, and spend five and one-half hours a day at the institute taking courses in machine-shop operation, steam-engine practice, elementary electricity, armature- and field-coil repair work on electrical machines, elementary chemistry, and batteries. It is interesting to note that Pratt Institute made a special effort to hold intact its student body of the regular courses, on the theory that the thoroughly trained mechanic or technician in service is many times more valuable to the nation than a private in the ranks. As a result of this effort, very few of the students of the day school dropped from the regular courses.

The William Hood Dunwoody Institute of Minneapolis began immediately on the severance of relations with Germany to serve as a recruiting station for the United States Engineers' Enlisted Reserve Corps, the United States Signal Enlisted Reserve Corps, the United States Quartermaster's

Enlisted Reserve Corps, the United States Civil Service Commission, and the United States Navy.

It also outlined a scheme for taking a census of mechanics and technicians for the state of Minnesota, which is now being carried out, and on the basis of which recruiting will go forward for every branch of the government service.

It made arrangements for bringing to Minneapolis, on the first of August, 425 recruits from the Great Lakes Naval Training Station at Chicago, and distributed them among the following classes in training at the institute: general electricians, radio electricians, carpenter's mates, machine-shop operators, gas-engine operators, blacksmiths, coppersmiths, cooks, and bakers.

The institute is training more than 200 novices in day and evening classes in telegraphy. Of these about 60 per cent are girls and women, this course being offered in response to a direct request from railroad and telegraph lines in the vicinity of Minneapolis. It is also giving some instruction in operating-foremanship work for a prominent local steel and machinery company, as this company has renewed the manufacture of munitions and needs operation foremen. The institute was called upon to select the most promising men and to train them in one process of which they are later to have charge in the shop. Director Charles A. Prosser in making a report to the secretary of the National Society for the Promotion of Industrial Education said:

We have 154 people taking radio work in day and evening classes. This group is made up of a number of different types. First, there are the amateurs with licenses who have enlisted in our first radio company of the United States Signal Service and have gone into that class to improve their speed. Second, there are other young men who have gone in to learn the work so as to be recruited into another radio company of the United States Signal Corps or into the naval service, and there are, in the third place, young men who have gone in with the idea of offering their services to the Marconi Company, either for land work or for duty on board the merchant ships which are being built.

Somewhere in the neighborhood of 500 mechanics and technicians have been sent into different branches of the government service by Dunwoody Institute. This number is made up in part of our own students from our school — particularly from the evening classes, although some of our day boys have gone — and in part of mechanics and technicians throughout Minnesota who have gone into the service through Dunwoody Institute, where we conduct a recruiting station and where we are recruiting into the service every Wednesday, applications being taken in the interim.

We have sent into the service 1 motor-truck company; 2 others are in process of organization. We are sending out 1 radio company, which is ready to go, and are about to organize another. We are also organizing 1 wire company, 1 baking company, and 1 company of cooks. In addition we have sent men to the Brooklyn Navy Yard and are sending men to the Puget Sound Navy Yard. We have also put men in touch with the Civil Service Commission and sent them into the service in this way.

The response of these and other colleges and technical institutes justifies as nothing else could their past claims that they train not only for the spirit of service but for the life of service.

The effect of the war on the college curriculum cannot be hastily measured. Institutions of collegiate grade are slow to make radical changes in the requirements for the bachelor's degree. Some have already shortened the college course to three years. Others have decided as a war measure that students ought to be through college by the time they reach conscription age. Some are offering opportunity for all-the-year-round work. Others are allowing war service to count toward a college degree. The English universities are already thinking of strengthening their courses in science and laboratory research, of giving more attention to modern languages, and of developing vocational courses.

Certainly in America there will be an immediate and greater demand for so-called "practical" subjects. It may be that one of the effects of the war will be the sharpening of the differentiation and an increase of competition between the idealistic and the practical groups of studies. This will be unfortunate. There should be no sharpening of differences of opinion. They had much better be dulled. There is no real necessity for antagonism between the cultural and the vocational subjects. People only *think* there is a need for constant justification of the one against the other. Such thinking has become a habit of mind.

The French have a way of saying that the cultural subjects are merely the moral conditions, the ethical history, and a judgment as to the ethical value of the world complex of vocational and economic life; for this reason any conflict between cultural and vocational subjects is impossible, and the more vocational education is developed, the more will the cultural aspects be needed and the more highly developed will they become. The French point out that what we term cultural subjects developed in two civilizations which were very highly practical, vocational, and militaristic; namely, Greece and Rome. They speak of the humanities as being essentially the abiding lessons of those civilizations which in vocational and military efficiency stood much higher above their fellows than Germany stands in those respects above contemporary civilization to-day.

Vocational subjects are direct-service subjects always. By their very nature they respond immediately to an emergency. The cultural subjects are more indirect in their effect. They could not be otherwise. I often wish we could get into the habit of speaking of liberal subjects in the sense in which this term was used in the older days of our colleges, when the term "liberal" implied that the subjects classed under this head were liberalizing; that is, they liberated, or set free, the minds, spirits, and bodies of men and women from prejudice, selfishness, tradition, passion, cruelty, and so on. I have never seen how one could *elect* culture, for it is always a by-product coming out of thinking and living. To study the language of an ancient people and to learn nothing of their government or ideals is useless. To study this government and these ideals of an older civilization and to see no lessons for the world of to-day is almost valueless. To study the past in terms of problems of human society is liberalizing.

New meanings of the realities of war are before us. New concepts of two great ideals of government confront us. New methods of making war more horrible strike our eyes with every news issue. New schemes for patching up human life that it may go forth again to battle or return to industrial warfares of peace are heralded every week. New societies for the relief of human suffering due to the war are chartered constantly. New alignments of political groups committed to reform are in the making. New groupings of nations not formerly allied stand before our eyes. New methods of combining activities of great corporate interests for government needs are published daily. New trade possibilities now latent are prophesied as being inevitable. New ideals and new ideas gathered in the trenches are appearing over battle lines for new governmental practices. New advances in the field of government control of prices startle us continually.

Out of it all there looms up a new science of chemistry, improved methods of transportation in the air, a still greater standardization of making industrial products, a new conception of government control of trade and industry, a system of government insurance for individuals and corporations, new concepts of legislative authority and action, and a score of other things all heading up into a new sense of nationalism, — and who knows but even a sense of internationalism!

Is it credible that education alone will remain unaffected by these world changes?

CHAPTER V

THE OPPORTUNITY FOR MANUAL AND HOUSEHOLD ARTS

A new spirit of teaching practical arts is upon us. The aims, materials, and methods of instruction in manual training, cooking, sewing, agriculture, and commercial branches are changing. They have been influenced by the vocational-education movement, and because of it practical arts in general education must justify themselves or else be put into the scrap heap.

The development and organization of differentiated courses in industrial, agricultural, and household and commercial arts adapted to junior and senior high schools — more particularly in connection with the education of children from 12 to 16 years of age — offers a new field of service to teachers of these subjects who, up to now, have been following methods unsuited either to the needs of vocational training or to the needs of general education. Already the set of wood and iron models taken from the Russian system of the early seventies has disappeared, and the sampler book in sewing has passed away. The era of the coat hanger and sleeve board in manual training and of the set of doll's clothes and models of undergarments is doomed, and the cooking outline which starts out with making cocoa in September and in the thirteenth lesson takes up the making of an angel cake will soon meet the fate of flowerpot holders, doll's aprons, and book agriculture.

But there is a great field for the practical arts in general education, — a field which no scheme of vocational training can possibly occupy. Each has its place. Vocational training is fitting young persons for profitable employment in chosen vocations. Practical arts in general education consists of varied lines of activity taken from the fields of agriculture, commerce, industry, and the household and taught in the school for the purpose of developing capacity to deal with concrete things and of arousing social and industrial interests in the workaday world.

In the early years of the child's life practical-arts work has a strong motor and social value. In the middle years, say from 12 to 16, it has a social and vocational-guidance value. The chapter entitled " The Field for Industrial and Trade Schools" gives a number of suggestions as to the work which boys and, to some extent, girls may offer as their service contribution in time of war. However there are fewer than 100 industrial and trade schools in the country. The majority of our youth are taking some practical-arts work as a part of general education in either the elementary or the secondary school, and surely these young people will want to do something in this emergency. And certainly the teachers of sewing, manual training, cooking, and agriculture will desire to do their part, not only because they can be of service at this time but also for the reason that through war-service work they will be able to improve upon the practical-arts work and make it conform to the new spirit. The whole spirit of the new methods is based upon getting away from individual models created out of the mind of a teacher and imposed upon an unsuspecting student body which follows a " course in models " in about the same way that it takes a course in arithmetic.

The present scheme of teaching practical arts is based upon the project plan and not upon the model or exercise plan. It no longer depends upon the teacher's course of study founded on tool exercises or logical sequence of processes. It now comes out of a need which is as clear to the student as it should be to the teacher.

The progressive teacher of manual training starts out with such a project, for example, as a garage. This involves making a sketch, working up a bill of materials, finding out the cost of lumber, cement, and so on. It involves work in concrete, laying the floor timbers, putting up the sides, laying out the roof, setting in the window and door frames, putting on the tarred paper or shingles or galvanized iron, and painting and staining.

The progressive teacher of domestic arts no longer thinks of catering merely to the personal decorative sense of young girls. She no longer has the girls spend the entire year making graduation dresses, or dish towels, caps, and aprons. She thinks in terms of quantity and in terms of social service which the domestic-arts work may render. She discovers that a hospital needs towels, aprons, caps, and bed linen, or that the orphan asylum near the school is sorely in need of children's garments, and then she tells of this need to the girls in her charge and the latter take up the problem in the same way that the boys take up the problem of building a garage. Each girl works in conjunction with others for a common purpose which all recognize as being worth while.

Progressive teachers of cooking are realizing that the idea of 20 cooking units in a schoolroom, where little batches of 20 model biscuits are made and where at the close of the lesson each girl has one of these small eatables, is far behind the practice of those manual-training teachers who are making drawing tables, benches, and looms, or laying concrete walks, building outdoor gymnasium apparatus, and so on. Some of the teachers have insisted on having a flat or tenement or entire house near the school, where girls taking domestic science can go to learn to make real beds that are really slept upon, to clean bathroom bowls that are really used, to cook meals that are really eaten by people who pay for what they eat, to shake real rugs that become really dirty, and to shop at stores where they come in contact with actual commercial conditions and at the end of a week discover that it really costs money to run a real home. A few teachers, and in time there will be many, desire to go still further. They believe that homemaking cannot be taught without having some babies around, and so they have established day nurseries in connection with the homemaking classes.

It is because of these things which have been mentioned in some detail that I was glad, as director of the Division of Agricultural and Industrial Education of the New York State Education Department, to send out a circular letter early in

April, 1917, to our manual-training and household-arts teachers, in which I stated that every teacher of manual training, sewing, or cooking should be thinking in terms of mobilization service, and that any teacher of manual training who was conducting his course of models, instead of thinking and working in terms of food production or industrial war service, was absolutely out of touch with the needs of the day. I advised him to turn his shop work over to home and community gardens, to increase the time allowance given to manual work, and help fill the cellar and pantry. I advised him to give his Saturdays and afternoons after school and even his vacation period to supervising garden work in the community. I said, furthermore, that any teacher of sewing who was not thinking in terms of Red Cross, and of mending, darning, and repairing, was as far away from the service idea as she possibly could be. I told her that with the increase in price of materials and with the scarcity of dress goods there would be necessary repairing and making over which would give her an opportunity to do some real things. I even told her that she might drop some of her sewing and help the cooking teacher in organizing classes in preserving. I told the teachers of cooking that if they were running through their outlines with no reference to the food shortage of next winter and the year after, they showed a lack of comprehension of the meaning of their jobs. I stated that the early summer and fall suggested lessons in preserving, while the winter season conveyed the idea of conserving. I asked whether they were planning to stop their work in June, before the canning season really began, and leave everything idle until school should open, when the canning season would be nearly over. I wondered what provision had been made in the community for using the summer service which they either had offered or, I hoped, were about to offer.

A few weeks later word came from England of how the manual-training teachers had been urged by those in authority to do garden work. A portion of these directions follows:

Surely wood and metal work have not the monoply of the educative value in manual operations. The harvesting of an orchard of fruit or a field of potatoes by a class of school children, accompanied by an enthusiastic teacher imbued with the right ideal of his work, can be made to serve other purposes than merely that of simple mechanical utility. A discussion started at first hand between child and teacher on such matters as variety and quality of produce, the destructive fruit pests and diseases encountered, the crating, packing, and distribution of produce, the weighing and measuring actually performed, the calculating of the value of produce and of labor, and a knowledge that the coöperative effort is in response to a call of England's need, would provide open-air lessons in nature study, geography, arithmetic, and civics quite as educative as any obtained in the elaborately equipped manual-training centers.

This is true, especially the phrase "a knowledge that the coöperative effort is in response to a call of England's need," which embraces the socializing value of the manual-arts principles, — a value which we often talk about and as often fail to attain.

Teachers of cooking, in this food crisis now upon us and the greater one which may come, ought to suspend temporarily some of their work in teaching children and turn their attention to teaching adults. To be sure the girl of to-day will be the mother of to-morrow, but the mother of the immediate to-morrow is also the mother of to-day, and the food crisis will be over, it is to be hoped, by the time the girls in our present cooking classes have grown into motherhood. These courses to adults should be intensive and in short units. The printing schools should print leaflets giving practical and helpful recipes to be distributed to the adults. If the women will not come to the school, then the schools should go to the women. By this it is meant that classes can be organized in churches, vacant stores, and settlements. In this connection it may be of interest to quote from the Leicester (England) education committee:

Arrangements have been made in connection with the local food campaign whereby the ordinary schemes of work at the domestic-science centers have been temporarily suspended and special short courses in cookery instruction provided instead. These courses have been designed primarily as a means of instructing as many women and older girls as possible in the method of preparing and cooking suitable substitutes for bread and potatoes. In addition to the rooms equipped for cookery instruction, those normally devoted to the teaching of laundering and housewifery are being used for this special work. The course is arranged to cover 4 lessons given on consecutive half days to each group of attendants, and at the conclusion of each course the women and girls attend one evening for a review lesson including a practical demonstration to which outsiders are invited. Leaflets have been prepared and sent to the schools for distribution. The children themselves write out the scale of rations as applied to individual families and take their copies home, thus becoming the active agents in the food campaign.

In Albany, New York, the regular work in cooking was discontinued early in June for the school year of 1917, and a special course of 10 lessons in food conservation was given at 4 domestic-science centers. The course consisted of 1 lesson in the preservation of eggs, 3 lessons on canning, 1 on making soap, 1 on butter substitutes, 2 on jellies and marmalades, and 1 on the drying of a number of agricultural products.

Not only may the domestic-science teacher go to adults by the way of churches or settlements, but she may go directly, — in the rural districts, at least, — with demonstration kitchens mounted on automobiles. In Lindsay County, England, for example, a domestic-science lecturer arranged an experimental course of lectures and demonstrations on economical cookery, and equipped with necessary utensils a traveling kitchen at a cost of $100. She covered each of the larger villages in the area selected, spending one day in each place, the morning being given over to traveling. In the afternoon, exhibitions of wheat-flour substitutes were arranged and demonstrations given that were based upon left-overs from her preceding evening's lesson. She also gave short talks on beekeeping, horticulture, fruit bottling, and so on. In the evening she gave a cooking demonstration.

The "van" used by the women of Long Island, New York State, consisted of a train of cars behind a steam locomotive, from which demonstrations were given in fruit and vegetable preserving. The County of Nottingham, England, gave similar demonstrations and in addition gave lectures to mothers on the necessity of taking unusual precautions with reference to the health of babies at this period. It was customary in much of the work in England to have an agriculturist go with the teacher and give talks on spraying, elimination of pests, and conservation of garden products.

One of the greatest services that the domestic-science teacher can render, whether she labors in rural or in urban fields, is the organization of canning clubs. The canning club enlists the services of women, girls, and even boys. It can be made as much of a social institution as corn husking and barn raising were formerly. But the teacher must, in most instances, move out of her domestic-science kitchen with its little gas stoves and quart saucepans. In the country district the equipment will be the stove in the village church, with a wash boiler, galvanized vat, washtub, or other vessel with a well-fitting top, which can easily be transformed into a home canner by making a false bottom with lifting handles. In a village or small city it may be necessary to beg, borrow, or buy the necessary cooking utensils, and to obtain free use of a vacant store, asking the local gas company to install, free of charge, some gas ranges. The boys will prepare the fruit; the women and girls will can it or dry it, as the case may be. To dispose of the product is a simple matter. It may be sold and the proceeds divided. It may be taken to the homes and the expense of producing shared.

In the city the domestic-science teacher serving as a leader of the canning club must watch closely the market and buy when the price is right, particularly when there is a surplus that may otherwise be wasted. It will be a new experience for many domestic-science teachers. It is a rather different proposition from canning a few baskets of strawberries, cherries, or currants in a classroom.

Naturally other containers than glass jars or tumblers will have to be used. In fact, the canning club after one season of experimentation is likely to resemble, with its larger and more efficient equipment, a miniature canning factory.

In Berkeley, California, the children of the entire city had a Jar Day, when they went out and collected every discarded and undesired jar. These were cleaned and sold and the money was turned into a " service fund." Many jars, also, were filled with surplus vegetable products to be used for the poor in the winter.

Of course the old drying methods of grandmother's days must be rejuvenated. Mr. Fred P. Reagle, supervisor of manual training in Montclair, discovered one of the old-fashioned evaporators and had a large number made up by the boys in his school and passed out to neighboring communities. Here is an old home industry which may be revived in the home or the community.

Mr. Reagle, in describing his evaporator, writes:

I was obliged to build something which could be used anywhere regardless of the availability of steam heat, electric fans, or coal. Furthermore, it was necessary to construct from common stock material and to use some stock stove. I hit upon the idea of using a common laundry stove which could burn either wood or coal. I made 20 frames, covered with galvanized wire, to hold the fruit. The control of the air circulation was obtained by means of an adjustable sliding door beneath the stove. The heated air passes around and over the stove and through the fresh food products, taking out the moisture and going out through the adjustable ventilator at the top. The evaporator has a capacity of from 5 to 8 bushels of fruit and vegetables a day.

Another activity for domestic-science teachers of more experience will be in the training of cooks for the army, or, as the director of the School of Practical Arts (Teachers College) believes, " in the training of people to train cooks."

The following quotation from a letter written by Sir Robert Blair of London to Superintendent Maxwell of New York City shows what was done in London:

In the summer recess, 1915, 264 of our domestic-science teachers volunteered part of their holidays in order to help in the work of training 2500 soldiers to cook and to meet the ordinary requirements in this line of the private in the field. The War Office drew men from different units from all over England and brought them to London in two great groups and paid 1/9 a day for the up-keep of the men. The soldiers were billeted in the school buildings and the preparation of their food formed the basis of the cookery instruction. Each group was taken for a period of ten days. The War Office was most appreciative of the work done by these domestic-economy instructresses. The War Office did not ask us to repeat this the following summer, although it was repeated to some extent in other parts of England. The War Office, however, did ask us to lend them 30 carefully selected teachers of cooking for the purpose of visiting army canteens and giving advice both on cooking and (what I believe is more important) on quantities used.

Still another service can be rendered by the cooking teachers, especially in our large cities and in our industrial villages. This service consists in giving meals to children who are in want. Of course at the present moment we see little need for this work, but the pinch of poverty has come upon England, France, and Germany, and our own land may not always be one of plenty. When the need arises, teachers should be prepared to furnish lunches to the children and possibly even breakfasts, to say nothing about suppers. The

Good posters have a great influence on civic life at any time. Now they are invaluable. War-service posters designed by Manual Training High School boys of Brooklyn, New York

Girls at work; mothers watching. Why should not both work in a community kitchen equipped with evaporators, large containers, proper stoves, and utensils for doing a real piece of work?

dislocation of many ordinary trades and lines of business, the taking from the home of the family's means of support, the increased cost of food and provisions, and the prevalence of sickness due to neglect may necessitate the feeding of children in school. In London the list of children to whom meals were given daily increased rapidly from something like 32,000 in July, 1914, up to 75,000 about the middle of September, 1914. Fortunately, however, as trade and industry became better adjusted there was a steady decline in the number of children that were fed, so that in May, 1917, there were only about 12,000 — the children then on the list being mainly the children of widows who were forced to go out to work. The number of meals provided per week in the schools of England in July, 1915, was 200,000. In a year this number had dropped to 120,000.

The drawing departments might well have their students design posters. Those designed by American illustrators for the first Liberty Loan were surprisingly ineffective. Only one stood out — that with the reproduction of the Statue of Liberty with the accompanying symbol and direct wording. Our enlistment posters have been crude, lacking in psychological appeal as well as in design. It is questionable whether recruiting is aided by a

picture showing a naval officer lounging under a
palm tree while in the distance a marine is seen
standing amid bursting shells on a battleship.
There has been and will be an opportunity for
students to design posters for Red Cross work;
for enlistment as farm cadets; for enrollment in a
home-service unit for girls, in community canning
clubs, in Boy Scout work, in school, home, and
community gardening; for patriotic meetings and
a score of other occasions. Good posters have an
almost incalculable influence on civic life at any
time. Within the last year there have been held in
many cities various competitions in poster work of
pupils with such subjects as " Red Cross," " Thrift,"
"Safety First," " Fire Prevention," " Pure Milk," and
" Liberty Loan."

There is plenty of work for the manual-training
teacher. Mention has already been made of garden
work, not so much in school gardens, however, as in
community gardens, for, like the canning-club work,
here is a splendid opportunity to bring adults and
children together. In a number of small cities in
the country where tillable land could be obtained,
the manual-training teachers directed a community-
garden project. The boys built the tool house;
the Boy Scouts took turns in acting as watchmen;
plots were laid out on a family or individual basis;

seed was purchased in bulk and distributed at cost; experts, hired by the day, plowed and harrowed the ground; stakes marking the plots were made in the school; and the manual-training instructors, or, as they were termed, the garden directors, spent their summer vacation in a useful service.

The manual-training teacher may help the Red Cross chapter in packing supplies into the boxes which his boys have made. He can be planning the hospital furniture which he may be called upon to make, as in France, where the boys built furniture for improvised hospitals and installed electric lights. He can be thinking how he shall, if required, make hospital-bed racks, cots, tables, and simple reclining chairs. Perhaps he may have to supervise, as have the manual-training teachers in England, the making of hand-grenade bags, chaff bags, dummy cartridges for the training of troops, or sand bags. In a single secondary school in Bradford, England, more than 1200 articles—including splints, crutches, bed-boards and rests, screens, rollers, trays, etc. — have been made in the manual-training department in one year. Perhaps in the early spring latrines can be designed and built for the farm cadets, as was done in the Newton (Massachusetts) school, or shacks for troops, as was done at Plattsburg, New York, by the boys from the Stuyvesant High School, New York City. The teacher may have his part to play in giving vocational training to maimed soldiers (see chapter on "Reëducation of the Disabled"), as all of the instructors in manual-training schools of the Dominion of Canada are now doing.

A manual-training teacher in Nashville, Tennessee, Mr. John M. Foster, has his boys make jig-saw puzzles, checkerboards, and bandage winders for the use of our soldiers in France. During the summer of 1917 he organized a boys' auxiliary of the Red Cross, and the group made packing cases according to official specifications. The organization included a shop foreman, a timekeeper, and a stock man. Lumber and other materials were contributed by local dealers.

Perhaps the manual-training instructor will coöperate with the teacher of domestic science, as male strength is needed, in providing comforts for the soldiers, such as socks and mufflers made on knitting machines, and in helping with the packing and crating. In this connection there is another quotation on the work of London children:

At the end of the first year of the war we began to organize efforts to provide clothing and other necessities for Belgian and Serbian children. In a few months the schools were able to furnish 10,000 complete kits made to the pattern and color and size supplied by the two embassies. It is reported that the making of these kits was one of the best exercises in planning, cutting, and sewing which the schools ever undertook, and probably nothing has done more to foster the school *esprit de corps* in the history of municipal schools since their origin, in 1870.

In France a number of schools, when the buildings were turned into hospitals, equipped either the entire hospital or a considerable number of beds at their own expense and by their own work. Hospital service was largely organized by these schools. One school would be responsible for the linen, another for mending, another for table service, another for cooking, and another for sending and receiving packages. A workroom established by the school girls in one of these hospitals had sent to the front in a year and a half 25,330 packages. One little village school of only 30 pupils in a short period collected 2542 eggs for the wounded soldiers and made socks and mufflers in addition. In another small district each of the schools specialized in some kind of work, one making up parcels for war prisoners, another knitting sailors' gloves, another making clothing for refugees, and still another providing candles for troops in trenches.

A small country school in the Midlands of England, in addition to weekly contributions of vegetables to the local hospital for wounded soldiers, has made 26 bed cradles and a dozen crutches, while the youngest boys have made splints.

A report from a northeast-coast district of England mentions manual-training centers where bed tables, toilet tables, bed rests, and clinical-chart carriers are made for the local hospital. Even the girls have made splints and bed tables. Of course hundreds of sand bags have been made in the schools.

The report closes with these significant words: "The effect of all this work has been most remarkable. Even districts where formerly little interest was taken by the children seem suddenly to realize the value of it all." This is what might have been expected, and what we in America may expect when we make our practical-arts work socializing, useful, and contributory to some great cause that the children see is worth while.

CHAPTER VI

THE WORK IMPULSES OF YOUTH

Since August, 1914, there have been presented to us new aspects of the relation of children to industry. Up to that time the only consideration for those who had the welfare of children at heart was the child himself; but with the war, the welfare of the child became tied up with the problem of the welfare of the country and its demands for service on the whole population. The endeavor to adjust these two in nice balance has resulted in experimental legislation or in action without legislation, both of which have often been of no genuine or lasting benefit to either interest concerned.

In America, in the first half of 1917, many of our states appeared to be following the lead of England in abrogating the compulsory-attendance law, urging the same reason for permitting children within school age to work in fields and factories. Everyone is familiar with the facts presented by farmer and industrial employer. In sections whose activity has been stimulated by the production of war products, such as Bridgeport, Connecticut, other industries and mercantile establishments have found it impossible to run as usual owing to the presence of munition plants, which attract an abnormal number of workers.

Not only is neighborhood business affected by the presence of war industries, but the farm shortage is aggravated; for the supply of intermittent labor, the kind demanded for berry picking, harvesting, and canning, is not forthcoming when the workers are offered steady employment in munition and textile plants. In 1917 many small canneries were threatened with the prospect of closing and letting the adjacent crops spoil in the fields; hence their call for schoolboys to assist them in cultivating and harvesting. This resulted in an unprecedented rush of children between 14 and 16 to obtain employment certificates, and a clamor from those below 14 to be allowed to leave school and go to work.

With the nation and the state urging farmers and food producers to make every exertion to increase the food supply, legislatures must render assistance in solving the labor-shortage problem. It need hardly be pointed out that the farmer cannot be expected to plant additional acres unless he is reasonably sure that it will be possible for him to have his acres cultivated and harvested.

England as early as September 1, 1914, was feeling the shortage created by the numbers of men enlisting, and every Local Education Authority was being besought by farmers and manufacturers to obtain modifications of the law which, generally speaking, held children in school up to 14 years. An order of the Board of Education to the Local Education Authority in Northamptonshire, answering such a plea, stated:

While the Board of Education have no power to give any general directions overriding the ordinary law with regard to school attendance and the employment of children, . . . a Local Education Authority is under no obligation to take proceedings in respect of nonattendance of a child at school if they are satisfied that there is a reasonable excuse for nonattendance.

The "reasonable excuse" was found in the overpowering clamor of farmers and munition makers who were suffering from lack of workers, as in Staffordshire, where the petition sent to the Education Authority by the bolt-and-nut manufacturers at Darlaston stated that owing to the enlistment of men in various branches of his Majesty's forces and because of the fact that the firms concerned were largely engaged on work of great urgency for the naval and military services, "it was desirable, in order to prevent delay in the execution of this work, that the school-attendance by-laws should be relaxed for the duration of the war so as to permit of the employment of boys over the age of 13 years."[1]

It cannot be stated too strongly that England has realized too late the practical impossibility of recovery for school of the children thus released, and the dangers to the nation of allowing the junior population to go into industry without supervision. There will be introduced into our legislatures in 1918 and later many bills which will parallel English action, and the various states must watch carefully to see that in their zealous attempts to increase food or necessary manufactured supplies they do not create and sanction disastrous conditions for the health and morals of the young.

Now action in regard to our schools may be of several types. First, there may be passed laws which abrogate the existing compulsory-attendance law; such legislation would be that permitting children below compulsory school age to leave school. Second, it is possible to have the existing laws interpreted so as to excuse absence from school, as in North Dakota, where the attorney-general in an open letter to school officers, April,

[1] Quoted from correspondence of the Board of Education to the Local Education Authority in Northamptonshire.

1917, interprets the section of the school law exempting children from school attendance in cases of necessity to apply to children of school age actually engaged in tilling the soil. A third type of action is that which suspends the compulsory-attendance law under certain conditions; such a law is the so-called " Brown Bill," chapter 689 of the Laws of 1917, New York legislature, to which reference will be made later. Action may also be taken in regard to shortening or lengthening the established school year, shifting vacations, and changing hours of session. For instance, the Bureau of Education at Washington has suggested keeping school open twelve months, and this advice may be taken in some localities; it is possible, also, that a continuation of the demand for agricultural labor of students may result in a different allotment of vacations in the apple- and peach-growing sections, so that students employed in harvesting may lose a minimum of school attendance.

Events moved very rapidly in the spring of 1917. We were called upon by national and state governments, by chambers of commerce and boards of trade, by bankers and railroads, to raise crops. We were told that America must be the pantry for all Europe and that, do the best that we might, we should not do overmuch. Obviously, with such

authority back of a movement for increased agricultural production, it did not take very long for
state boards of agriculture and state departments
of education to respond, to say nothing about the
propaganda set forth by settlements, women's clubs,
the Y.M.C.A., the Boy Scouts, the National Security League, the Women's Patriotic Service League,
and a score of other organizations, that put a
psychological persuasion into the situation which
was hard for school authorities and school children
to resist.

The following data relative to the action of
a number of the states were compiled by the
National Child Labor Committee. In general the
data showed no provision made for supervision,
for physical examination, for wages, or for definition of "passing grade." In some instances there
were even no age limitations.

California. During continuance of state of war, state
board of education with approval of governor may reduce
school term to six months when necessary " for the planting or harvesting of crops or for other agricultural or
horticultural purposes."

Indiana. Letter from state superintendent of public instruction to county superintendents, April 10, 1917, saying
in part: " It is my wish and order that you permit such
high-school girls and boys, and also such eighth-grade girls

and boys as may care to engage in Home Projects work looking toward the increase of our agricultural output, to engage in such work and to receive therefor full credit on the school records, provided this work is done to the satisfaction of the county agent and the county superintendent."

Plan formulated later by principals and state superintendents for supervising, certifying, and accrediting such work did something to stop a general exodus, but came too late to do much good.

Illinois. State superintendent wrote to local superintendents, April 10, advising that all boys eligible for working certificates be excused from school May 1 and receive a working certificate upon assurance that they have employment on a farm or in a garden, credit to be given for work upon guarantee that summer months have been spent in farming or gardening.

Kansas. State board of education advised local school officials, April 17, that it would " approve granting a full year's credit to pupils who have passing grade and who find it necessary to withdraw from school before the end of the school year either to enlist in the military service or actually to engage directly in food production."

Maine. Boys 16 and over excused from school attendance, June 1 to October 31, for work on farms under supervision of Y. M. C. A. official. (See chapter on " Farm Cadets.")

Maryland. Superintendent of schools, Baltimore County, in open letter to school officials, May 11, authorizes the employment on farms of "boys and girls who are old enough to be of real productive value." On days when not so employed they are required to attend school. Children over 13 who have attended school one hundred days during the year may be employed without permits ; those who have not attended one hundred days must have permits. Children under 13 must have a permit, "which should not be issued to a child who is too immature to do work for which the permit is asked." Permits issued for twenty days or less may be renewed upon application of parent.

Similar plan was discussed by state board of education but not approved on ground that it might lead to abrogation of the laws on child-labor and school-attendance.

Missouri. State superintendent of public schools wrote to local officials April 13, suggesting that they "excuse at once from high school all boys over 14 years of age who will go to farms and work. Give them full credit for their year's work at the end of the school year, with the standing they have at present. Have the boy who gets the credit give evidence satisfactory to you as to his work on the farm. Include boys who live in the country and boys who will go to the farm to work. Extend the same privilege to girls where you deem it advisable."

New York. (Referred to later in this chapter.)

North Dakota. Attorney-general in open letter to school officers, April, 1917, interprets section of school law exempting children from school attendance in cases of necessity to apply to children of school age actually engaged in tilling the soil.

State superintendent of schools in open letter to school officials, April, 1917, recommends that schools should not open earlier than October 1, with a spring vacation of four or five weeks, and that the school be kept open through

June and July when there is less and cheaper farm work to do. "This would make available, and with a minimum loss of school time, some 5000 of the older boys at a time when labor is scarce and wages are high."

Pennsylvania. State board of education, April 19, issued circular letter stating that farm and garden work should be considered valid excuse for absence from school, and for children 12 and over in good standing such work should be credited in lieu of school attendance.

New Jersey. State board of education sent out a circular letter to superintendents and principals in which it was stated that credit towards graduation might be given in place of school work during the time a pupil was actually engaged in farm work as a member of the Junior Industrial Army, or while called out in the service of the state or of the nation as a member of its organized military forces. (Boys and girls over fourteen years of age are allowed to enroll in the Industrial Army in the agricultural or home-garden or the girls' service division.)

Possibly no great harm was done by the action of these state officials and state boards. Yet the action affords food for thought; and perhaps the best way to bring about reflection is to pass immediately, without comment, to a quotation taken from the London *Times* of July 19, 1917, — a quotation which gives a picture of the end of the road on which some of us in this country started in the spring of 1917.

The reply, last week, of Herbert A. L. Fisher, Minister of Education, to a deputation of the Committee on Wage-earning Children was sympathetic and not merely a common-form shelving of the issue. The deputation asked for legislation restricting the labor of school children out of school hours. The extent of the evil was indicated by the deputation, but it is doubtful if even the educational public know how widespread and deleterious it is. On October 5, 1915, we pointed out that nearly half a million children between the ages of 12 and 14 years were receiving no education, or no education worth having, and that all of these were at work which led nowhither at the very age when their moral and physical development was at stake. Since then the conditions which we condemned have passed from bad to worse. Many thousands of children under the age of 12, under the ages of even 10 and 11, are at work, and willingly at work, since the younger the child, the more readily it responds to the demand for helpfulness. Mr. Fisher cannot but realize the evil of this exploitation of young children by parents and tradesmen. It is an evil affecting not only the efficiency of school life but our whole economic system. There never was an economic need for this child labor, and the Board of Education admitted in their circular to local authorities last week that there is no economic need in rural districts for such labor even now. This circular was a letter from the National Service Department and dealt with the pressure on education authorities in rural areas to release boys and girls under 12 for service on the land. The letter definitely states that, in view of the labor released from the army and the number of women now available, " it would appear that there should be no necessity for such a serious interruption as is contemplated of the education of the nation's children."

This should suffice to determine the policy of the rural-education authorities. But the position in towns is even more urgent, and Mr. Fisher and the government might give additional powers to local authorities to deal with the labor of children in full-time school attendance. It was certainly a mistake in the legislation of 1913 to make it possible for the street trading of such children to receive official recognition. But street trading is not the chief cause of anxiety. Another is the employment of little children by shopkeepers and distributing agencies before school, in the dinner interval, and after school. The local authorities should be empowered to forbid all employment for wages of children under 12 and to restrict within very narrow limits the employment of children at school under 14.

Naturally Mr. Fisher must not overburden or imperil his bill, or interfere with the labor necessary for the war. He cannot be expected to change the face of England in a moment. But he can strike deep without disturbing the organization of society. He can transform from below by ameliorating the conditions of very young children. The country is ready now for changes that seemed Utopian two years ago. By means of nursery schools the nation is dealing at last with the raw material that is to be the England of to-morrow. The same principle should be followed in the case of children between the ages of 6 and 12 years. The physical welfare of these children is of the first importance. Yet between these ages thousands, through the carrying of heavy weights and other means of overstrain, are receiving life-long physical injury. All efforts for educational reform are being balked by their employment. The elaborate scheme of the Half-Time Council, which was reported in our last issue, depends, as indeed practically all of the reform schemes and Mr. Fisher's own proposals depend, on the physical efficiency of the children. The deputation asked that provision should be made for the education of children abnormally employed during the war.

Out of all the literature which has been put forth on the relationship of children to industry in war time it would appear that Dr. Claxton, United States Commissioner of Education, most adequately states the fundamental principles, in his circular letter to the educational authorities of the country issued in June, 1917. Portions of his letter bear directly upon employment of children in time of war. Other portions are closely related to statements in other chapters. It is well worth quoting in full:

It is of the utmost importance that there shall be no lowering in the efficiency of our systems of education. Schools and other agencies of education must be maintained at whatever necessary cost and against all hurtful interference with their regular work except as may be necessary for the national defense, which is, of course, our immediate task and must be kept constantly in mind and have right of way everywhere and at all times. From the beginning of our participation in the war we should avoid the mistakes which some other countries have made to their hurt and which they are now trying to correct.

If the war should be long and severe, there will be great need in its later days for many young men and women of scientific knowledge, training, and skill; and it may then be much more difficult than it is now to support our schools, to spare our children and youth from other service, and to permit them to attend school. Therefore no school should close its doors now or shorten its term unnecessarily. All young men and women in college should remain and use their time to the very best advantage, except such as may find it necessary to leave for immediate profitable employment in some productive occupation or for the acceptance of some position in some branch of the military service, which position cannot be so well filled by anyone else. All children in the elementary schools and as nearly as possible all high-school pupils should remain in school through the entire session.

When the war is over, whether within a few months or after many years, there will be such demands upon this country for men and women of scientific knowledge, technical skill, and general culture as have never before come to any country. The world must be rebuilt. This country must play a far more important part than it has in the past in agriculture, manufacturing, and commerce, and also in the things of cultural life — art, literature, music, scientific discovery.

Russia and China are awakening to new life and are on the eve of great industrial development. They will ask of us steel, engines, and cars for railroads, agricultural implements, and machinery for industrial plants. They will also ask for men to install these and to direct much of their development in every line. England, France, Italy, and the central empires have thrown into battle a very large per cent of their educated and trained men, including most of the young professors and instructors in their universities, colleges, and *gymnasia*, *lycées*, and public schools. Their colleges and universities are almost empty. The young men who would under normal conditions be receiving the education and training necessary to prepare them for leadership in the future development of these countries are fighting and dying in the trenches. All these countries must needs go through a long period of reconstruction, industrially and in many other respects. Our own trained men and women should be able and ready to render every possible assistance. It should be remembered that the number of students in our universities, colleges, normal schools, and technical schools is very small as compared with the total number of persons of producing age — little more than one half of 1 per cent. The majority of these students are young men and women who are becoming more mature and fit for service. The older of the 60,000,000 men and women of producing age are growing more unfit and are passing beyond the age of service. It should also be remembered that the more mature the young men who volunteer for service in the army, the more valuable their services will be.

Therefore a right conception of patriotism should induce all students who cannot render some immediate service of great value to remain in college, concentrate their energies on their college work, and thus be all the more ready and fit when their services may be needed either for war or for the important work of reconstruction and development in our own and other countries when the war shall have ended.

All schools, of whatever grade, should remain open with their full quota of officers and teachers. The salaries of teachers should not be lowered in this time of unusual high cost of living. When possible, salaries should be increased in proportion to the services rendered. Since the people will be taxed heavily by the federal government for the payment of the expenses of the war, teachers should be willing to continue to do their work, and do it as well as they can, as a patriotic service, even if their salaries cannot now be increased. All equipment necessary for the best use of the time of teachers and students should be provided, as should all necessary increase of room, but costly building should not be undertaken now while the prices of building material are excessively high and while there are urgent and unfilled demands for labor in industries pertaining directly and immediately to the national defense. Schools should be continued in full efficiency, but in most instances costly building may well be postponed.

During school hours and out of school, on mornings, afternoons, Saturdays, and during vacation all older children and youth should be encouraged and directed to do as much useful productive work as they can without interfering with their more important school duties. This productive work should be so directed as to give it the highest possible value, both economically and educationally. For children and youth in schools of all grades there will be need of more effective moral training, and provision should be made for this. While the war for the safety of democracy is in progress, and when it is over, there will be greater need for effective machinery for the promotion of intelligent discussion of the principles of democracy and all that pertains to the public welfare of local communities, counties, states, and the nation. To this end every schoolhouse should be made a community center and civic forum with frequent meetings for the discussion of matters of public interest and for social intercourse.

One phrase in Commissioner Claxton's letter is especially significant. It is *This productive work should be so directed as to give it the highest possible value, both economically and educationally.* In this whole question of children and industry in war time, we are brought face to face with several facts. The first is that industry, both agricultural and manufacturing, will demand the services of children. Second, that organizations like state and national child-labor committees, which have fought for the welfare and development of American children, will continue to oppose all attempts to break down the school system through relaxation of the enforcement of compulsory-education laws, or to break down the labor laws either by giving young children special permits to work or by exempting certain establishments from the laws limiting hours of labor. Third, that the children themselves will desire to work rather than go to school. The comparatively high wages which will exist during a war emergency will call them as can no course of study. Fourth, that families whose earning member or

members are off to war, and who feel in addition
the higher cost of living, will look upon their children as being a possible added source of income.
And fifth, that school authorities will thus stand
amidst half a dozen fires. Some will back against
the wall and say: " I don't believe in closing the
schools," " Under no conditions will the child-labor
laws in this state be relaxed," " The war hysteria
makes me enforce child-labor laws more vigorously
than ever," "Children have plenty of time to garden
after school." Others will, under pressure, lose their
heads, and shut their eyes to the fact that children
are working illegally. Some may seek for a "reasonable excuse," and they can find plenty of such excuses by referring to the action in England. Still
others will go on peacefully without thought or
action one way or the other. But the rest, and it
is to be hoped that their numbers are legion, will
try to discover some means of making this emergency count in an educational way. Here are some
of the factors which enter into the situation.

In the first place, children like to work, that is,
outside of school, and these work impulses of youth
ought to be organized to contribute to the educative process. It is readily enough granted that
they have not been in the past. In fact, these
work impulses have been exploited for private gain.

Now, on account of the war, they are aroused to a high pitch, and we ought to be able to organize them in connection with the new work opportunities for higher economic efficiency as well as for higher social efficiency.

In the second place, it is doubtful whether we can much longer continue the policy of increasing the regular attendance of youth at school without giving some consideration to the educative value of labor. The educative process taken in its largest sense goes on for twenty-four hours a day. It concerns health, character, mental capacity, citizenship, and useful work. To most people the educative process merely centers around the schoolhouse, and such think of education in terms of schooling. To them, to increase the number of years that youth is obliged to go to school is to increase the number of years given over directly to the educative process. But the child goes to school for about five hours a day for five days in the week for about thirty-six weeks in the year, and in this time he deals largely with books; and many find it a reasonable excuse, because they are " going to school " and " getting an education," to avoid any useful work. Now some kinds of work are wholesome and educative. Most farm work comes in the class of useful and profitable employment. When the hours are not too long and the factories and stores are sanitary and the pay is reasonable, work in these places may be profitable to youth. Because this is not always the case is no reason why we should not attempt to make it so.

It would seem that educators now occupy a strategic position from which they may exert a tremendous influence in the direction of standardizing the work of juveniles in terms of the deepest social significance, and a good start in this direction may be made in meeting the war emergency. The subject is so large and the previous discussion of it so limited that we have not very much background on which to work, and it is not advisable at this time to do more than merely hint at some possible procedures.

First, why not have the rural schools for children up to 12 years of age open early in September and close the first of August, and make provision for stopping the school work of the youngest children during the winter months in those parts of the country where it is difficult for them to reach school? Why not organize classes in dandelion digging, berry picking, currant picking, and even, once in a while, weeding, by having a series of field and harvesting days under the direction of the school teacher with the coöperation of the parents? Why not have able-bodied boys in these rural schools released from book work in April and remain out of school until the first of November, and then require them to attend school faithfully for six days a week during the rest of the year? Why not have the boys between 14 and 16 drop out of school in June and July to pick small fruits and berries and to work in vegetable gardens? Under certain conditions, in regions where such service can be used, — which is not often, — they might stay out in September to pick fruits and gather small crops.

Of course it is to be expected that the answer to all of these questions will be a most emphatic No. Yet they have not been set up primarily because the farmer tells us that he needs labor, but rather because it is felt that boys need labor; that is, useful labor.

Second, why not devise in cities a scheme of part-time education for youths between 14 and 18 years of age who will be needed in the war emergency in factories and stores, as well as for youths who need useful labor as a part of the educative process? If the war falls heavily upon us in America, we shall find that these children will go anyway. We shall find that the male teachers who teach them will be drafted. We may even find — although it is hoped not — that the school buildings will be taken over for military purposes. But I am not thinking particularly of war needs. I am thinking of child needs. England proposes to reintroduce into the school system children who are now abnormally employed in the war. It further proposes to develop out of its war experience, on a large scale, the part-time and continuation-school idea. It is reported that in France a part-time and continuation-school bill will be introduced in 1918.

Now why not take hold of this whole matter of juvenile employment in a constructive way? As long as war is upon us we have better opportunity than ever of passing through the legislature part-time and continuation-school measures. We have at the same time, out of all the experience of England, every opportunity to formulate laws for the employment of juveniles in a way which will not break down the educative process, but will rather build it up; and above everything else we ought to enforce strictly all child-labor and compulsory-education laws which we have on the statute books. We may modify them, if we will, to meet war emergencies, if it appears absolutely necessary, but better than that, we may reconstruct them in the interests of the educative value of labor when combined with proper rules and regulations relative to the employment of children.

Furthermore, why not find some way of bringing agriculture into the educative process of the city boy? Would it not be a good idea to establish country branches for city schools, providing for the older boys a winter course of study in the science of agriculture, together with the ordinary academic branches of secondary-school education, followed in the spring by practice in an agricultural training camp? Later on in the season they would go out to work individually or in groups for farmers. (See chapter on "Farm Cadets.") The older of these boys would make admirable assistant teachers and supervisors for the younger group of 14-year-old to 15-year-old boys who would be sent to these camps after schools had closed. We cannot much longer avoid the question of bringing agriculture to the city boy or, rather, taking the city boy to agriculture; and the past summer's experience with city boys working on farms brought forcibly to our attention the advantages of a closer relationship between city children and country life.

Mention has been made of the modification in 1917 of the school-attendance law of New York State. Three sections of the act by which these modifications were made are quoted in full, as they represent legislative action as well as discretionary powers of the state educational official.

Section 1. The provisions of Art. XXIII of the education law, relative to the compulsory education of children, may, in the discretion of the Commissioner of Education, be suspended for the period between the first day of April and the first day of November of each year, or any portion thereof, during the time that this act shall remain in effect, for the purpose of aiding and performing labor in the cultivation, production, and care of food products upon farms and gardens within the state. Such suspension shall be subject to such conditions, restrictions, and limitations as may be imposed by the Commissioner of Education, and shall be subject to rules and regulations to be prescribed by him. In case of such suspension, provision shall be made for the welfare and protection of the children affected thereby, and during the period of such suspension and while engaged in such work, they shall be under the supervision and direction of the school authorities of the city or district in which they reside. . . .

Section 4. A pupil in the public schools or in any state school or institution who is relieved from school work and is engaged satisfactorily in agricultural service during the present school year shall be given credit for the work of the present term without examination, on the certificate of the person in charge of such school or institution that his work therein up to the time of engaging in such service is satisfactory. A pupil in such school or institution who engages in such service during the present school year shall not incur any loss of standing or credit on account of such service. All pupils in public schools who are candidates for college-entrance diplomas or other credentials to be issued to them at the close of the present school year shall be granted such diplomas or credentials on the certificate of the principal of the school that their work up to the time of engaging in such service is satisfactory. The Regents of the University shall make rules for the purpose of giving credit to pupils in the public schools who have been in attendance at school during the present school year and who have left the schools for the purpose of rendering agricultural or industrial service.

SECTION 5. The Commissioner of Education shall cause appropriate certificates or badges to be prepared and issued to pupils in the schools of the state who shall perform satisfactory agricultural or industrial service under rules and regulations of the Commissioner of Education.

It will be noted that the compulsory-attendance law was suspended only between certain periods and at the discretion of the Commissioner of Education, and for the sole purpose of permitting children to labor in the cultivation, production, and care of food products upon farms and gardens within the state.

This bill did not authorize the employment of girls in general domestic service. No provision of the labor law was repealed, suspended, or modified, and the provisions of the labor law relating to the employment of children in canneries or in any factory or mercantile establishment still remain in force. It is true that a bill suspending temporarily in whole or in part, at the discretion of the

Industrial Commission, provisions of the labor law in relation to any employment in the state passed the two legislative bodies, but this was wisely vetoed by Governor Whitman.

It will be further noticed that the children thus employed within the dates mentioned are to be under the supervision and direction of the school authorities in the city or district in which such children reside. The Commissioner of Education thereupon issued certain regulations relating to children who might be employed within the compulsory school ages. A brief summary follows:

Boys only, 15 years of age and above, residing in cities.

Boys only, 14 years of age and above, residing elsewhere than in a city.

Girls, 14 years of age, and above, residing outside of cities, may work at home in the district in which such girls reside, or at a place sufficiently near such girls' homes as to afford supervision by their parents.

No child shall be employed or permitted to work on farms and gardens until such child shall obtain a farm-garden permit.

No child shall receive a farm-garden permit who does not present to the issuing officer the written consent of his parent or guardian and who is not found to be physically competent to perform the labor proposed.

In the chapter on "Our Colleges and Technical Institutes" reference was made to resolutions of the Board of Regents and to the fact that the State Education Department formulated a plan for enlisting and placing high-school boys on the farms, for directing and supervising the work of such boys, and for the adjustment of school credits. With this resolution in mind the Commissioner of Education sent out, on April 16, the following letter to all school superintendents and school principals of the state.

To meet the present national emergency, the New York State Education Department, after careful consideration, issues the following regulations concerning matters that vitally affect the interests of the pupils of the secondary schools of the state.

1. The June Regents' examinations will be given as previously announced for all pupils who remain regularly in school and also for pupils who may enlist for service and who wish to take the examinations and are situated so that they can do so. For the latter class the time requirement will be waived.

2. Announcement is made to all the schools of the state that any pupil who enlists for military service or who enlists for and renders satisfactory agricultural or industrial service will be credited with the work of the present term without examination on the certificate of the school that his work up to the time of enlistment is satisfactory.

3. Candidates for college-entrance diplomas who are in the graduating class of 1917 will be granted the diploma on certificate of the principal that their work up to the time

of enlistment is satisfactory. The average standing will be computed on the basis of the examinations already passed.

4. Appropriate certificates will be prepared to be issued to those pupils in the schools who shall enlist for agricultural or industrial service and who shall present satisfactory evidence of such service.

5. That all other questions regarding conditions affecting the 1918 high-school class be held in abeyance to await developments.

It is believed that principals, teachers, and pupils in all secondary schools of the state will appreciate the vital importance of prompt action in the present crisis and that each will esteem it a privilege to "do his bit" for the common good.

As soon as the schoolboys of the state knew of this letter, they all seemed to hear very suddenly of jobs on farms, but some, rather unfortunately, failed to continue to hear this call when the end of the school year came and they could no longer receive school credit for work on the farm because, of course, school had closed. It being likely that there would be the same general tendency for the boys to discover work on farms about the first of September when the schools open, it was thought well to have a clear understanding of the conditions of release of boys for farm work in the fall. Of course a great many boys were out of school during May and June and continued to work all summer on individual farms or in camps with other boys, but "slackers" wanted to stop as soon as they received their school credit, and the same slackers might be just as slack in returning to school, hence the following letter issued by the Commissioner of Education on August 11, 1917:

To Superintendents, Principals, and Boards of Education :

In answer to many inquiries as to releasing boys for farm service this fall, and in response to the appeal of the Food Supply Commission, which states the imperative need of such labor as the youth of this state can give in harvesting the crops, I would urge the educational authorities of the state in those sections where the need exists to make all possible provision for the special tuition of those pupils who may, under the labor laws of the state and the compulsory-education laws, legally engage in such service. Such special instruction, either after hours or in holiday periods, may be the special patriotic contribution of some teachers to meet the need which seems at present to demand whatever coöperation the school authorities can give. This will be most easily arranged by limiting the enlistments, as far as possible, to the upper classes, and by arranging for work in relays, so that the period of absences may not be unnecessarily long. We ought not to remit in the slightest our educational requirements and disciplines, nor take children or youth out of the educational processes, but we ought to do all that we can, on the other hand, to make it possible for the boys of proper age and strength to perform this service when it is of real public necessity.

The department, wishing to coöperate to this end, makes the following determination, effective until November 1, 1917:

The time of study requirements for admission to the Regents' examinations, in January and June, 1918, may be waived in the case of any pupil who presents evidence that

a. He was regularly registered in school at or near the beginning of the term in September, 1917. (Boys already at work at a distance from the school may, with the permission of the local principal, register by mail.)

b. He was released by the principal from school for agricultural service.

c. He was actually and satisfactorily engaged in needed agricultural service while absent from school.

This privilege should be interpreted conservatively. School authorities should excuse pupils from this service only where the need is urgent and where it is possible to maintain such supervision that certificate of the facts can be made from certain knowledge.

During the summer and fall of 1917, schoolboys from Maine to California responded to the nation's call for increased food production. Other seasons of scarcity of labor, with the shortage of farm and garden products and resultant high prices, are doubtless before us. Indeed, we are told that for five years at least we are to continue to feel the stress of labor shortage due to war and other conditions. The United States Boys' Working Reserve, through state councils of defense and state and national departments of labor and agriculture, will

continue to issue proclamations calling upon youth
to serve the nation. Legislatures will pass or amend
laws permitting absences from school for industrial
and farm service. State educational officials will
issue edicts interpreting legislative action. Schools
will devise methods of giving school credit for useful
service. Boys will again leave school to earn and
serve. Parents will continue to speak with pride of
the earning of their lads or complain about their
treatment. Farmers will recall their first experiences with city boys. Everything will center about
products, laws, rules, school credits, and dollars.

Few of us will think of the deeper significance of
what is behind. We shall hardly realize that the law-
makers have thought only of a possible increase of
acreage under cultivation, or increased production
in factories; that the farmers and the manufacturers
had visions merely of good labor at a low figure;
that the parents saw only an opportunity for a
"change for the boy"; that the boy had in mind
only a spending account and release from school.

We shall forget our unscientific experiments, the
light handling and selfish exploitation we have
given to that wonderful possession of youth — the
work impulses. And the question we should ask
ourselves is, What educational justification have we
for this service which the boys have rendered?

CHAPTER VII

ORGANIZED BOY POWER VS. MILITARY DRILL

The war has already brought about drastic economic changes in Europe. The recall of men from the trenches to perform a more useful professional and industrial service behind the lines has demonstrated the importance of the supporting civilian army. From the viewpoint of the individual, nothing can equal the supreme sacrifice of a life. "What good," wailed a Yiddish woman on the East Side of New York City, " is a free country to me if my Abie is killed?" But in the judgment of the nation the garment worker, Abie, who is drafted into service in the army is of no greater value than his friend the skilled machinist who is allowed to remain in his present occupation. The military exemptions of men in European armies, the adoption of the selective draft in the United States, are acknowledgments of the equality of the military and the civilian occupations indispensable to military activity. To include in our educational law such a recognition, adopting a measure permitting the substitution of types of vocational training for military training, is but to follow the lead of the national government in declaring such exemptions a military necessity. New York State has made a beginning in this direction.

In 1916 the legislature enacted the so-called "Welsh-Slater" bills, making military and physical training compulsory in the secondary schools of the state for boys above 16 and under 19 years of age. Such military training is to aggregate not more than three hours each week between September first of each year and June fifteenth of the next. The law further provides, within the limits of appropriation, for the establishment of military camps with attendance of from two to four weeks. While the operation of these camps and, indeed, the introduction of military drill, have been imperfectly carried out, owing to the lack of suitable state appropriation to carry on the work on the necessary and large scale for a working-boy and schoolboy population of 240,000, it is the intention of the Military Training Commission to insist on the requirements of the law.

The law as passed in 1916 contained a significant clause relative to the excusing of boys exempted by the Military Training Commission. It was felt by the critics of the bill that, although the law requiring military and physical training was a movement in the right direction, it left much to be desired. The ambiguous word " exemptions " is one subject to fine distinctions. Furthermore, it was felt that the law was essentially one of discrimination. The schoolboy of 16 to 19 was in an exclusive military class, set apart, in his capacity to be trained for national service, from the employed boy of the same years.

It is not easy to justify the selection of the high-school pupils of the state as the only young people who shall be the recipients of military training. The report of the New Jersey commission appointed to study military training in its relation to high schools covers this point admirably.

The duty of the common defense is one which belongs properly to all who are physically capable, and none should be deprived of the opportunity of qualifying himself, if such opportunity is offered to any, to perform this duty effectively. It cannot be claimed that the boys of the high schools are exceptional, and that they are the only ones who can receive this instruction profitably. If there is any advantage in it, all boys equal in age and physique to high-school boys can receive it with equal probability of profit. If it is claimed that the reason for providing this instruction for the high schools is that the pupils can best afford the time for it, it must be answered that very many of these derive an income from labor out of school hours which enables them to attend school. These are as worthy of exemption from military instruction as those who leave school because they lack the ambition to continue their education, or because they are compelled to do so by circumstances. Whether this instruction is compulsory or optional with pupils of the high schools, if required or offered at all, it should apply to all boys, out of school as well as in school, of prescribed ages and strength.

Military training and service, if they are necessary, are obligations of citizenship, not of education alone.

It is difficult to contemplate with satisfaction or even complacency the social cleavage which is bound to result from a system of military instruction which is applied to high-school pupils and not to other boys. To assign or reserve the privilege, or duty, or obligation, however it is regarded, of preparing to fight for the country to the better-educated class is just as repugnant to democratic ideals as was the practice in days long gone by of leaving it to the nobility. To select high-school pupils for this training is open to the same objection as would be a plan of selecting adults for actual military service solely on the basis of their occupations or professions — a plan which would receive no consideration.

Military authorities admit that the fundamental aim of every form of military training must be to cultivate physical health and strength. As Dr. George Fisher, secretary of the Physical Department, International Committee, Y.M.C.A., and a member of the New York State Military Training Commission, puts it, " In the training camps in England it takes a full year to get the men in condition after they enlist. England's experience in this war indicates that the big problem is not primarily the training of the men on military tactics or drill, but conditioning the men. Therefore the lesson to us should be to discover what methods can best be used to put and keep men in good physical condition."

If any evidence of the accuracy of this opinion were needed, it is necessary only to consult the records of the United States War Department. The following table shows the number of applicants for enlistment in the United States army, furnished by the several recruiting districts, together with the number accepted or rejected in said districts, fiscal years ending June 30, 1911 to June 30, 1915:

	TOTAL NUMBER OF APPLICANTS	ACCEPTED		REJECTED	
		Number	Per cent of total applicants	Number	Per cent of total applicants
Total for five years	747,704	157,043	21	590,661	79

In order, therefore, that all citizens may be properly trained and prepared to perform effectively all their duties, no matter what they may be, we recommend and strongly urge that the necessary steps be taken to provide for all the schools of the state a complete and thorough system of physical training. This system should be compulsory for all pupils, and should include carefully selected exercises adapted to the different ages of pupils, and designed to protect their health, stimulate bodily functions, and promote physical strength. It should apply to all girls as well as boys. It should aim to prevent bodily abnormalities or deformities, or to correct them if they are found to exist. It should include personal and community sanitation, first aid in emergencies, bandaging, and all forms of instruction in personal safety. It should encourage outdoor activities. It should provide abundant games for all pupils in which group activities are prominent, and in which appeal may be made to the spirit of competition. It may include those features of military drill which properly serve the purposes of physical training, but which must be regarded as subordinate to these purposes. It may even include practice with the miniature or the service rifle, if such practice is regarded as necessary to develop steadiness of nerve, bodily control, and accuracy of sight. In the case of such exercises the educational error does not lie in their use, but in the exaggerated military purpose which they are made to serve. All the features and exercises of the thorough course of physical training which we recommend should be intimately connected and interrelated, on the one hand with the moral or character-forming instruction of the schools and on the other with the complete provisions for medical inspection which have already been made compulsory by law.

Now boy service should be democratic. The exemptions, whatever they are, must be made on a basis of the equality of the schoolboy and the boy engaged in wage-earning. A boy should not be excused from his rightful preparedness training because he happens to be employed as a bell boy in a metropolitan hotel. Such work is not industrially productive, nor could any devised system of military equivalents make it a substitution for personal contribution to national preparedness.

In the spring of 1917 the legislature amended the law to include all boys — a drafting of the boy

power of the state in much the same way that the
European nations in conflict make provisions for
the full utilization of man power. An additional
amendment, as stated in chapter 49, Laws of 1917,
reads:

Such requirement as to military training may, in the
discretion of the commission, be met in part by such vocational training or vocational experience as will, in the opinion
of the commission, specifically prepare boys of the ages
named for service useful to the state, in the maintenance
of defense, in the promotion of public safety, in the conservation and development of the state's resources, or in
the construction and maintenance of public improvement.

The commission was given power to establish
a bureau of vocational training. This, through
careful inspection of the work of boys of the ages
named in industrial, commercial, and agricultural
pursuits, will determine the types of vocational
training or vocational experience which, in the
opinion of the commission, specifically prepare
boys for service useful to the state.

Such a bureau would, under normal conditions,
appoint a few inspectors and investigators to study
conditions in order that carefully laid plans might
be made for carrying out the provisions of the
amendment. But war emergency in the matter of
food supply gave the Military Training Commission

an opportunity to organize at short notice one branch of military-equivalent service, that is, the farm-cadet unit, and it extended an offer of assistance to the Food Supply Commission to organize farm-cadet bureaus in each of the six military zones of the state. Through these the Military Training Commission has been useful in placing boys upon farms, and in following up such farm service with a view not only to determining its merit as an equivalent or partial equivalent for military service but also (with the coöperation of church and business organizations, the Y. M. C. A., and the Boy Scouts) to giving the task which these boys have been doing on the farms its proper place in relation to the physical, mental, and social ideals which lie outside the hard and often unfamiliar round of field work.

Important as this farm-cadet service has been in the matter of looking toward increased production, a more significant work to be developed by the Bureau of Vocational Training is that of interpreting the spirit and purpose of the amendment already referred to, which states that provisions for the military-training requirement may be met in part by certain types of vocational training or vocational experience. The whole program of physical, military, and vocational training is most significant, wholesome, and far-reaching. It is a program of universal training which will be serviceable for war and peace alike — a program which will require every boy to prepare himself to offer some service in case of need, and which stamps that service as equally patriotic with the narrower military service in which most of the world's supreme valors have been recorded. As John Finley, Commissioner of Education in New York State and one of the members of its Military Training Commission, puts it:

In this amended law we have a program providing, on the one hand, for the defensive training of the soldier and, on the other hand, for the effective mobilization of the resources of the nation in training boys for vocations — which training of itself exalts and identifies as patriotic service all the effective activities of our everyday life. It is a constructive provision for what would have to be done otherwise in time of need through exemptions.

England has had to reach such a program through an exempting provision in her plan of coöperative service. France has had to come to it by taking men from the front for service behind the lines. Germany is finding it necessary, in the midst of war, to organize her entire man power.

It is most important that this vocational training or experience should be *conscious* service. The boy who offers it must clearly understand why it is accepted in part for the required military drill.

To fail to inform him is to take from his military equivalent the educational value given it by the law.

Dr. Finley, in his inimitable way, expresses this conscious service as it might apply to an adult loyal citizenship:

I make this idea graphic to myself by thinking that every man has an imaginary uniform (as every German soldier and French soldier had in waiting his green-gray or his blue and red uniform), an imaginary uniform of his own measurements always in readiness in home or shop or office or in some public locker, that he may don at call of his community, state, or nation, or perhaps at world need, when under compulsion he goes to vote, to pay his taxes, to fight against dishonesty, inefficiency, or waste, to inform himself upon public questions, or upon his public duties, just as one studies tactics in order to help in his country's defense, or goes to school as an alien to learn the language and institutions of a new land, or joins his neighbors in promoting the health of his community, in conserving resources, in securing means of healthful recreation for children and youth, in improving the highways — when, in short, he performs any one of a hundred offices that are required of him as an efficient unit in an organized society.

Those who oppose military training in the schools will be less critical of its requirements when they are open to the broader interpretation suggested in the amendment of 1917. Those to whom the thought of training the young in the carrying of arms is repugnant may here see the educative value of universal service. Early in the war Germany discovered that the relation of industrial to military service is 2.7 per cent; that is, to keep one man in the field, nearly three men must work in those occupations, industrial and agricultural, which support the nation at war.[1] It is the work of the New York Military Training Commission to select as a partial military equivalent such vocational training or vocational experience as will, in the present or in the future, serve the nation.

What shall the nature of this work be? The decision is to be left to the state Military Training Commission. It is easy to weed out those occupations which have no national productive or defensive value, but there will be difficulty in selecting those vocations which may or may not be military equivalents, which under war conditions may belong to the work of an industrial or agricultural army, when in peace they seem entirely separate from national service. Such an occupation is that of a junior telegraph operator, which is not of a productive nature, and yet a very necessary factor in war equipment. The case of a printer's apprentice

[1] Authorities differ widely; some even state that the ratio is now as high as one to eight.

is less equivocal. Only in rare cases could his work be accepted as a partial substitute for the required service.

The problem is not to separate the useful from the useless occupations, but to discriminate between those which may be called upon to serve the state and those which have value only to the individual. All the productive and useful occupations are not socialized; and in selecting those which are partial equivalents for the required military drill, we have to make a distinction which has not been hitherto considered in economic classification of occupations.

To Ruskin's generation his suggestion that Oxford and Cambridge undergraduates should serve short periods as builders of roads for the empire seemed little short of fantastic. And yet the turn of time may even bring about the confirmation of this anomaly.

There is a parallel between the economic substitution for military drill and what William James in an astonishingly pertinent essay written in 1910 calls the " Moral Equivalent of War."

If there were, instead of military conscription, a conscription of the whole youthful population to form for a certain number of years a part of the army enlisted against *Nature*, . . . the military ideals of hardihood and discipline would be wrought into the growing fiber of the people. . . .

A farm camp is not merely a recreational camp, although it may re-create the city youth in terms of country life. A group of Long Island Food Reserve Battalion boys with the working impulse strong

Even hoeing requires special training and was one activity in the pre-vocational course in agriculture given at the concentration and training camp for Junior Volunteers of Maine

Instruction in mechanics, electricity, friction, heat, horsepower, etc. nowadays centers about an automobile. This work at Wentworth Institute (Boston, Massachusetts) has a military-equivalent value

To learn a trade in an essential industry is to enlist in national preparedness. A corner of a Buffalo (New York) vocational school, teaching plumbing and steam fitting

To coal and iron mines, to freight trains, to fishing fleets in December, to dishwashing, clothes-washing and window-washing, to road-building and tunnel-making, to foundries and stokeholes, and to the frames of skyscrapers, would our gilded youths be drafted off, according to their choice, to get the childishness knocked out of them, and to come back into society with healthier sympathies and soberer ideas. . . . Such a conscription, with the state of public opinion that would have required it, and the many moral fruits it would bear, would preserve in the midst of a pacific civilization the manly virtues which the military party is so afraid of seeing disappear in peace.

Liberty Hyde Bailey, author and farmer, formerly director of the New York State College of Agriculture, in a chapter of a recent book on " Universal Service" expresses in concrete terms a similar thought from the angle of the open country.

Not of all persons will be required the same duty. What one is, that shall one give. Society will learn of every man and woman what these gifts may be. Some day it will be expected that every able person will report himself, at determined occasions, for definite service, without pay, in one or more of the following privileges, and other privileges, under orderly management and recognized public authority :

1. To clean up the earth and to keep it sweet, — streets, roads, paths, byways, vacant lots, stream banks, woods, fields, and all open, or public, properties and public works. The clean-up days now becoming popular are the beginnings. Of course this does not mean that the work of street-cleaning

departments and the like is to be taken over or interfered with; but there are times for special house cleaning. If every person felt it devolving on him to help in keeping the earth decent, he would be likely to exercise a proper restraint in befouling it; and as charity begins at home, so should his restraint begin on his own premises, even extending to the parts out of sight of the public.

2. To take part in the construction of halls and premises for community activities.

3. To aid in the making of beautiful and public places accessible and to protect them. Every community with a rural environment, and practically every small city, has a near-by area that could be reserved and opened by coöperative action of the people, — days set aside when paths should be made, bridges built, retreats discovered, trees and streams put in shape, insects destroyed. Such reservations are not really public until the people volunteer to help in them.

The farther places, the real backgrounds of the race, will some day be opened as well as reserved, and made of much use to very many people besides casual visitors and sightseers. We shall learn how to project whole counties and cities, and even larger units, into the making and keeping of them in a way that is not yet visioned. This can be accomplished as easily as armies can be sent into the field, but it will require a type of organization at which we have not yet arrived. It will be worth while to develop public-service armies.

4. To demand the freedom of the earth for its inhabitants, under proper recognition of vested rights. The conception of the freedom of the sea has had an interesting

evolution, — the escape from the old sea fear, the long years of piracy, the buccaneers, letters of marque and reprisal, treaty ports, smuggling, and all the rest; finally has come the demand of equal opportunities for all and the open door. We must have the open door to fields and shores, to commanding hills that should not be exclusive property; find trails and walks and avenues to places the people ought to know. All this requires exploration, tramps far and near, maps, propaganda. All scenic parts will be marked. The public shall know all good places.

5. To protect the products of the earth; and to protect the earth itself. The products to which I now refer are those not the property of individuals, — the birds, the beasts, the fish, the vegetation. The bird sanctuaries now so well accepted are good beginnings, as also the wild-flower preservation societies, the nature-study groups, and many others; but the individual is not yet sufficiently impressed with this feeling in his own action.

To protect the earth is to save its fertility. This is the fundamental conservation. Not all persons can participate here, but every citizen can be mindful of the necessity of it and aid in creating public sentiment. I wait for the coming together of new organizations or societies that shall have for their purpose the conservation of fertility. These will be much more than agricultural and rural organizations, and their work need not be technical or occupational. They may include all persons, and the discussions and interests may run the range of man's relation to land.

To leave his piece of earth more productive than when he took it is the obligation of the good farmer, for there are constantly more persons to be supported. In the large sense every one of us is a farmer, for the keeping of the earth is given to the human race. We begin to understand vaguely what relation the good keeping of the land bears to national questions.

6. To keep the public health, — to protect it by keeping one's body well, by taking care to commit no nuisance, to contaminate no source of public infection, and to lend one's self to participate in the correcting of abuses.

To be physically fit and uncomplaining is a public duty. Maybe we shall find ways to demand physical training of the people as effective as that afforded by military training but without its sinister intentions.

Society will take over unto itself the oversight not only of physical training and of providing that children shall be well born but also more and more the oversight of the treatment of disease, as a public necessity. We shall train the sound to care for the unsound.

7. To come with personal succor as well as with money and goods in time of flood and disaster, to visit the sick and the afflicted, to relieve the poor and unfortunate. We shall learn how to organize the vast resources in men and women who are willing but do not know how, who are undiscovered and untrained, yet who could be shaped into a great army of assistance.

8. To respond promptly to the call of societies or groups that act in the public interest; to participate in the many neighborhood coöperations.

As an illustration of the manner in which a military equivalent may be determined, an illustration has been taken from some agricultural

activities. Before considering the military equivalent in farm work it is necessary to give a brief
description of the basis upon which the Military
Training Commission will probably work in this
matter. The basis, in brief, is the "man work
unit" idea as developed by Dr. George F. Warren,
Professor of Farm Management, New York State
College of Agriculture.

A man work unit is the *average* amount of work
accomplished by a man in ten hours. A horse
work unit is the *average* amount of work accomplished by a horse in ten hours. For New York
conditions, *an acre* of the following crops represents the man and horse units indicated below.
In a majority of cases the numbers which follow
are based upon cost accounts. In some instances,
where data were limited, the results are more or
less an estimate.

MAN UNITS	HORSE UNITS	CROPS
6	6	Corn for grain husked from shock (New York method)
3	5	Corn for grain husked from standing stalks (Western method)
5	6	Corn for silage
3	5	Fodder corn
6	6	Sweet corn
10	10	Potatoes
4	5	Field beans

Man Units	Horse Units	Crops
10	10	Cabbage
20	7	Tobacco
50	8	Hops
15	12	Roots (field beets, mangels, etc.)
2	3	Buckwheat, oats, barley, wheat, spelt, rye, field peas, and mixtures of these
1	1	Hay for cutting, alfalfa, clover, timothy
2	3	Oat hay, millet, and other grains cured for hay
15	5	Apples, bearing, when cared for in a commercial way
3	1	Apples, bearing, when little or no care is given
15	5	Other tree fruits, bearing
2	1	Fruit not of bearing age
20	5	Berries
3	5	Peas for canning factory
1	1	Seeds (alfalfa, clover, timothy)
3	5	Sorghum
12	6	Cotton
10 to 35	2 to 10	Truck crops

For live stock listed below, the man units and horse units are as indicated.

Man Units	Horse Units	Live Stock (Basis of One)
15	2	Cows, ordinary dairy (majority grades)
20	2	Cows, pure-bred dairy (majority pure-bred)
15	15	To be added per cow when milk is retailed
2	0.1	Heifers, calves, bulls, steers, and colts when running loose
2	0.1	Steers or other cattle, fattened or only wintered
0.5	0.05	Breeding ewes and bucks (covers work on lambs)

Man Units	Horse Units	Live Stock (Basis of One)
0.2	0.02	Other sheep or lambs, fattened or only wintered
3	0.05	Brood sows (covers work on pigs till weaned)
0.5	0.1	Boars
0.5	0.1	Other hogs raised during the year
0.15	0.02	Hens and other poultry
0.15	0.02	Pullets, etc., raised during the year (covers work on cockerels)
1.0	0.05	Bees, per hive
6	0.0	Day-old chicks per 1000

In order to interpret the man-work-unit idea in terms of the military requirements of New York State that 16-year-, 17-year-, and 18-year-old boys are to participate in such military training or as a partial equivalent may offer farm experience or farm training, it is necessary to translate the number of hours required for such military instruction into crop values or, to use the term already understood, man work units.

Since there are 288 days or 41.1 weeks in the required military-training period (September first to the fifteenth day of June next ensuing), a boy must drill 123.3 hours. This represents on the average 12.33 man work units.

For example, if a boy grows 1.2 acres of potatoes or takes entire charge of .6 acres of berries, including cultivation, picking, marketing, etc., for a period

of one year, he has spent in productive agricultural
work the number of hours required for military drill.

MAN UNITS	MILITARY EQUIVALENT
6	2.05 acres corn for grain husked from shock (New York method)
5	2.46 acres corn for silage
6	2.05 acres sweet corn
10	1.233 acres potatoes
4	3.08 acres field beans
10	1.233 acres cabbage
20	.616 acres tobacco
50	.246 acres hops
15	.822 acres roots (field beets, mangels, etc.)
2	6.16 acres buckwheat, oats, barley, wheat, spelt, rye (field peas and mixtures of these)
1	12.33 acres hay per cutting (alfalfa, clover, timothy)
2	6.16 acres oat hay, millet, and other grains cured for hay
15	.822 acres apples, bearing, when cared for in commercial way
3	4.11 acres apples, bearing, when little or no care is given
15	.822 acres other tree fruits, bearing
2	6.16 acres fruit not of bearing age
20	.616 acres berries
3	4.11 acres peas for canning factory
1	12.33 acres seed (alfalfa, clover, timothy)
3	4.11 acres sorghum
10 to 35	1.233 acres truck crops

In the case of live stock a boy can do all the man
work necessary in caring for 6 heifers or 82 hens or
approximately one ordinary cow in the time which
another boy may be giving to military training.

The exact military equivalents are shown in the second column.

Man Units	Military Equivalent
15	.82 cows, ordinary dairy (majority grades)
20	.616 cows, pure-bred dairy (majority pure-bred)
2	6.16 heifer, calves, bulls, steers, and colts
2	6.16 steers or other cattle, fattened or only wintered
0.5	24.66 breeding ewes and bucks (covers work on lambs)
0.2	61.6 other sheep or lambs, fattened or only wintered
3	4.11 brood sows (covers work on pigs till weaned)
0.5	24.66 other hogs raised during year
0.5	24.66 boars
0.15	82 hens and other poultry
0.15	82 pullets, etc., raised during the year (covers work on cockerels)
0.3	41.1 hives of bees
6	2.05 thousand day-old chicks

Military equivalents as related to farm training or farm experience appear to be much easier to develop than those concerning mechanical training and experience, especially where the work of 16-year-old to 19-year-old boys is concerned.

At the present writing there seems to be on the part of the public no very clear understanding of the government's policy relative to exemption for persons who are performing industrial and farm service. If it is difficult to determine an exemption policy for drafted men, it is very evident that when boys of 16, 17, and 18 years of age have become industrial drifters and have not decided upon a vocational career, the determination of a military-equivalent policy for them is a problem much harder of solution.

Again, a study of boys' occupations reveals the fact that only a very small proportion of those "above the age of 16 years and not over the age of 19 years" who are at work in our cities are engaged in occupations that will specifically prepare them for service that has productive or defensive value. Under the auspices of the Committee on Vocational Help to Minors the Bureau of Attendance of New York City made an extended survey, during the summer of 1915, of 5000 children who had left school between the ages of 14 and 16 and entered industry. Because of the vast amount of labor involved in tabulating the data that were collected, a random sampling was made of 150 boys and the same number of girls from each of 5 attendance districts. The 5 districts were selected to represent as nearly as possible the general character of the city. Each of these 1500 cases, 750 boys and 750 girls, was given a key number so that when the information was tabulated it would be possible to identify each case and verify the information. Of the 750 boys 546 were within the ages designated by this statute, 188 were under 16 years of age and 16 of the boys were 19 years old.

Half of the boys were either errand-messengers, clerks, or office boys. There were 213 in the errand-messenger service, 107 clerks, and 55 office boys. Another 100 were either stock boys, wagon boys, or packers and wrappers. The largest trade group was made up of 14 boys who were classed as machinists' apprentices, and the second largest trade group, that of electricians, had but 5 boys.

The departments in which these 750 boys were working indicate the nature of the employment. There were 265 in offices, 134 in the shop departments of factories, 165 in shipping and delivery departments, 92 in salesrooms, 35 in stock rooms, 31 in other departments, and 28 cases where the investigator had failed to secure this information.

A careful study of the work done by each of the 750 boys resulted in the selection of 32 who seemed to be doing work that might give them the specific training indicated as essential. The result of this study can be summarized under the headings of the trades the boys were learning.

Blacksmith. The one boy apprenticed to this trade had been working in the shop for seventeen months, was earning $13 a week, and was perfectly satisfied with his work. So he was likely to continue until he learned the trade.

Brass worker. Of the two boys of this group, one had served twelve months and the other twenty-four months at the trade. They earned respectively $5 and $6.50 a week and both intended to remain at the trade until it was learned.

Carpenter. There were two boys serving as carpenter's helpers. With one it was simply a temporary position. The other had been working at the trade for a year, and although he was receiving but $4 a week, he intended to remain at the trade.

Electrician. Three of the five boys working at this trade had been employed for over eighteen months as electricians' helpers. The other two had had four months and two months respectively of such experience. The five all expressed a determination to remain long enough to learn the trade.

Ship fitter. The one boy in this group, although out of school over a year, had been working at the navy yard but two months.

Locksmith. With only ten days' experience this boy was ready to quit.

Machinist. The average time spent by the 14 boys classified as machinists was less than three and one-half months, and not one of the group had worked as long as a year. Three were running drill presses, 1 was cleaning the wheels and pipes of a feather-bone machine, 2 were not employed. Most of these were dissatisfied and looking for other work. A boy who had been working eleven months on a screwing machine, 1 who had worked nine months repairing autos, and 1 who had worked eight months as a machinist's helper — 3 out of the 14 — had worked long enough at the trade to know that they liked it, and expressed the intention of learning the trade.

Plumber. Three of the four boys classified as plumbers' helpers had worked over a year and a half at the trade, liked the work, and expected to follow it. The fourth boy was using it as a temporary job.

Solderer. The one boy in this line was dissatisfied with the job and with his pay.

Sheet-metal worker. The one boy serving as a tin-roofer's helper had worked for the firm for a year and was perfectly satisfied with all conditions.

There seem to be 14 of the 750 boys who had been working long enough at a trade and were sufficiently pleased with the prospects for the future to make one safe in saying that they would probably complete their apprenticeship — although this conclusion may not be justified. These 14 were distributed as follows:

Blacksmith	1
Brass worker	2
Carpenter	1
Electrician	3
Machinist	3
Plumber	3
Sheet-metal worker	1
Total	14

This study of Mr. Chatfield's shows that not only were very few of the boys between the ages of 16 and 19 receiving vocational experience that would train them to be useful to the state in the maintenance of defense or in the other interests of the state as outlined in the bill, but also boys of these ages are likely to change their work rather frequently. There were 184 of these 750 boys who had been out of school between three and four years when this study was made. Of these 184 boys 41 were still working at the job they first had when they left school, 47 were on the second job, 41 were on the third job, and 13 had made eight or more changes.

I know of no study which more clearly points out the "blind alleyness" of the employment of children. However, some of us, including Dr. David Snedden of Columbia University, feel that a better term than "blind-alley occupations" would be "occupations involving juvenile employment." To us the evil of errand-messenger, clerk, or office-boy service is not that boys wander into or are thrust into a line of work which may be a blind alley, but rather that *no provision is made in the public-school system for giving the boys a short preparatory training helpful to them in this temporary service, and that no training which would help them to get out of such work is given them in the office, store, or factory.* If society would frankly recognize that there are juvenile employments and that boys might well work in them while they are juveniles and yet be trained through such work, and apart from such work in continuation schools, to discover themselves and to prepare themselves for other work, we might develop a constructive educational program.

This study certainly shows the waste of the boy power of the state and proves conclusively that there is need for the state to grapple consciously with the problem of conserving its youth; and when one reads this summary of an accurate and previously unpublished report, one is led to believe that William James, John Dewey, Liberty Hyde Bailey, and John Finley are right in their contention that there should be a mobilization of the boy force of the state looking toward conservation of the boy power that it may lead into training for skilled work, into citizenship, into sturdy health, and into right living.

CHAPTER VIII

RED CROSS AND OTHER COMMUNITY WORK

Thoughtful people are becoming disposed to criticize the present methods employed in many of our sewing, cooking, and millinery classes. It is felt that the girls in these classes, through the work which they do, think of themselves first, last, and all the time. They spend time on embroidery to cater further to decorative instincts long established by custom without much thought as to artistic values. They spend half a year making graduation dresses which they may wear before admiring parents. They copy the latest fashion in hats without thought as to utility or beauty. They knit feathery neck pieces and neglect stocking darning. They laboriously sew by hand articles which had better be made on a machine.

Our girls must learn to think of others than themselves. Their sewing and millinery must get away from the individual-problem idea. Of course girls must learn to sew by hand, especially when the home in these days teaches so little in the way of hand sewing. But after they have learned to

sew by hand, they should not continue to use
hand sewing on work that should be done on a
sewing machine. Of course it is wise to train
girls to make some of their own clothing, but to
make this clothing without regard to study of tex-
tiles or adaptation to personal needs or the eternal
fitness of things is not in accord with the educational purpose of our schools, which is to train
personal character as well as to develop skill in
domestic arts. When the family hosiery needs
darning, and the small children of the family need
clothes, and the schoolgirl needs a middy blouse
or a school uniform, it is unwise to spend so
much energy on continuing a type of domestic
art which lacks the socialized appeal necessary
to conform with modern social needs and modern
industrial methods.

The teachers of household arts are beginning
to see the need for reform. Many are bringing
into the school life such problems as the mending
and darning of the family clothes; cooking school
luncheons; managing day nurseries for babies of
working mothers; making table and bed linen for
hospitals; making jams and jellies for charitable
societies. Such teachers have welcomed the opportunity offered by the present war to forward the
new idea of socializing domestic-arts work. They

have been impatient of the dilettante work which
they formerly did when their girls practically
wasted hours of school time in making things
which could be bought for less than the cost of
materials, to say nothing about the cost of time
of the girls themselves, who are in school but a
few years at best — years when they should be receiving instruction in subjects which have real
training values. These progressive teachers have
desired that their girls develop more speed; that
they receive training helpful in meeting the actual
trade conditions in dressmaking and millinery
shops; that they learn to work together on some
common problem which all may see is worth while
and for a purpose which is larger than themselves.
Red Cross work has given these teachers the opportunity which they sought. They believe that
the Red Cross work during the war may easily be
converted into community work after the war is
over. Hospitals, charity organizations, orphan asylums, and homes are always with us. The great
appeal now, obviously, is Red Cross work. The
permanent appeal is always the need of the home
and the community.

An activity which has been very general throughout the country, as well as in France and England,
has been the voluntary contribution of the work of

women's organizations to the Red Cross Society. The making of hospital supplies belongs more peculiarly to women than do many forms of war work, and it is easily incorporated into the sewing courses of our elementary and secondary schools. A feature that makes it especially adaptable to schools is the standardization by the present business manager, under whose direction blue prints, photographs, and written and pictured specifications have been prepared.

Those of us who are interested in the methods employed in vocational schools to turn out standard products appreciate the benefit to the girl of learning to work from well-planned directions and of turning out a product exactly corresponding to specifications. It is believed that this manner of doing the work holds an educational value which entitles it to a place in the sewing course of every school. Both technique and speed elements are necessary for the condition of need which the Red Cross is meeting. As pupils are called upon to respond to this demand for quantities of garments and hospital supplies, as well as for accurately made articles, they will become trained in speed and accuracy while rendering a distinct service to their country.

In the state of New York about 3000 girls in sewing classes began work for the Red Cross on

March 1, 1917, under the direction of Anna Hedges Talbot, state specialist in girls' vocational work; the work being done voluntarily by both schools and pupils. To obtain materials, arrangements were first made with local Red Cross chapters; but in many places the lack of a chapter or its lack of funds prevented the coöperation with the schools, and material was supplied by liberal contributions from women's clubs, which realized the necessity of making use of the offer of the girls' services, thus causing more work to be turned into Red Cross channels than would have been possible without this financial aid. In organizing the work the various localities sent an authorized school person, generally the teacher of household arts, to confer with the Red Cross people as to what articles were needed and how they should be made, and to bring back to the school written specifications, paper patterns, and models. In many places the teachers took a course of instruction under some Red Cross nurse specifically qualified to give sewing instruction.

In this careful way the schools proceeded, and within six weeks returned reports to the State Education Department showing that every kind of article which was needed, from the simplest surgical dressings to the most carefully finished surgeon's gown, had been made by about 3000 girls working on an average of one or two hours a week during their regular school time. That none of this work had to be ripped or done over when it reached the Red Cross headquarters reflects credit on both girls and instructors.

One comparatively small sewing class in the vocational school at Mount Vernon, New York, filled a box for the Belgian Relief, according to Red Cross specifications, as follows:

18 hot-water-bag covers	9 pairs slippers
54 sheets	9 convalescent gowns
36 pillow cases	36 pairs socks
27 wash cloths	18 pairs bed socks
27 pairs of pajamas	18 bath towels
36 hospital-bed sheets	36 face towels

In addition this class shipped in a few months over 2000 separate articles to Red Cross headquarters; as, for example,

75 children's dresses	14 chemises
149 tampon bags	403 body bandages
224 baby bootees	42 eye bandages
219 ward shoes	373 bathing suits
76 hospital nightshirts	12 air cushions
62 crocheted trench caps	77 pneumonia jackets
597 slings	50 bath towels
19 petticoats	

All the schools of the state inquired if they might go on with this work when the schools opened in September. Schools which were not able to do the work in the spring were ready to begin on the first day of school in the fall. The work, however, has hitherto been neglected except in the curriculum of schools which have vocational courses, so that only girls electing domestic arts have had the opportunity of doing it as a part of their school program, but there is no reason why it should be limited to these girls. Those who are taking academic courses in high schools — and they greatly outnumber the vocational students — should have a chance to render service through the schools. In this connection it is well to say that the burden of doing productive work in war service should not be limited entirely to students in vocational courses. It will be a mistake to throw the burden of useful service upon a special group and in this way help develop the notion that those who take classical courses have nothing to do but look on, while those in vocational courses are to do the work.

Voluntary after-school clubs were organized in a great many schools, but no voluntary work can be systematized or directed so well as courses incorporated in the curriculum, and it is suggested to the schools of the country that special Red Cross courses be offered and that all girls be expected to devote a few hours a week to the work.

The following quotation from Édouard Petit's book " De l' école à la guerre " on what the normal schools of France are doing ought to be enough to inspire our American girls.

The girls of the normal schools of France are working very hard, knitting, sewing, making hospital supplies, in the intervals of their school work ; also acting as laundresses, secretaries, bookkeepers, etc. They are not old enough to be nurses. In addition to the work for the armies, they give a part of their time to work for other students. They are providing for the girl students of the normal schools in the invaded districts, many of whom were obliged to make long journeys on foot, clad in summer clothes, with no chance to carry even a change of clothing with them. The school at Fontenay appealed to the normal schools for aid for its students ; other appeals followed, some from schools in the districts from which the invaders were driven out. Very soon in all the normal schools of France girls were cutting and sewing, providing new garments, or garments from their own supply, to be sent to the towns in the north of France. Some of these supplies are held in reserve for the towns that are still to be liberated. One teacher writes : " Our young girls are glad to come to the aid of their fellow students who are not known to them but who are coming to seem nearer as I have them learn about the schools, read the letters that are received, etc. Anything which makes real and tangible the responsibility of this friendly help ought to be encouraged."

As the need arises, our secondary-school girls will respond in like manner.

The preparation needed to initiate Red Cross work in any large way in the schools of a state is considerable. There is a good deal of organization and consequent detail connected with it. The domestic-arts teachers of a school district or county ought to be called together and instructed in the minutiæ of garment-making and surgical dressings. With the blue prints, photographs, and written specifications already issued by the Red Cross headquarters at Washington these teachers could then work out a full set of directions for each article which would be specific and graphic. These could be printed by the state printer or, better, by the boys in a vocational school. In addition, moving-picture reels of processes carried on according to the most modern methods of workroom procedure could be shown to those who have not been in contact with present-day modes of work.

In order to excite interest on the part of the community in rural districts where this work has not as yet penetrated to any extent, moving pictures of processes of making surgical dressings, pajamas, surgeons' gowns, or children's dresses could be exhibited as illustrating what other sections of the state are already doing. These moving pictures could be taken of girls at work in an up-to-date New York City factory, and the reels could be either purchased outright or rented from an educational-film company. In Washington the Department of the Interior has a number of reels which have been put at the disposal of the Red Cross, and will make more if the occasion demands. Slides too could be made showing special operations, special garments, and special methods of arranging work. When public interest has been aroused at a public meeting in a small center, the school will find it easy to take up the work and push it forward. The person in charge of the work would have to keep in constant touch with the Red Cross headquarters as to the needs for garments and hospital supplies, as well as to the changes that from time to time have to be made in the kind and quality of supplies. A chart could be made of the capacity as to equipment and number of pupils, and the present grade of their working ability, for each place where a school is located. Brief reports could be sent to a state director from these schools as to what they could make, when they could make it, and when specified articles could be finished. Thus there would be a line out from a central supervisor to each school in the state where pupils are old enough to do any work of this public-service nature. Along this line would travel the information as to what was being done and what would be the next thing to be done.

Knitting by hand is one of the occupations which many girls and women are taking up. One drawback to hand-knitting is that it takes a good deal of time, and in the case of socks, at least, the results of amateur work may be uncomfortable to the wearer. It is suggested that schools put in knitting machines. One school at Yonkers, New York, has such a machine. It enables its operator to finish a sock every twenty minutes, or 12 pairs in an eight-hour day. It is possible to knit wristlets and sleeveless sweaters on these machines. The Vacation War Relief Committee of New York City has been responsible for the sale of 980 of these machines, on which over 85,000 pairs of socks have been made during the past year.

A letter written to me by Mettie B. Hills, Director of Girls' Work in Troy, New York, relative to her Red Cross work is so full of human interest and gives in such detail the excellent methods which she employed that I quote it in full. It will serve as suggestive material for other equally enthusiastic and competent teachers.

My office has been turned into a cutting room. Girls are now at a large table cutting hospital bed shirts with just as little waste as possible. Smaller girls are snipping the few waste pieces, and one little girl at the end of the table is filling a fracture pillow with the snips. In my machine-sewing room the girls are making hospital bed shirts. Each girl has a different operation. The shirts move through the cutting room to this room and from one machine to the next just as they do in a factory. They finally reach the inspection table, where they are inspected as they are folded, and an inspection card is placed in the pocket. They are then piled up for that final inspection which I give every article before it goes to our stock room. Here we hold all articles until we have enough to make the moving worth while, and then they are taken to Red Cross headquarters in the city truck. The chairmen of each Red Cross division of our local chapter are notified beforehand that things are coming and they are at headquarters to receive our work and sign for it. I tell you, it is a big day for all when the school work is turned in. I hear about it for weeks afterward.

The girls do not stay at one operation. As soon as they are ready, they are promoted to the next. [And in this connection may I call the reader's attention to the chapter which brought out the new spirit of teaching the household arts?]

The little jacket which is hanging in my clothespress is only the beginning of a big piece of work which I expect to push during the winter, a piece of work which I believe will do more to standardize the girls' work than anything we have yet done.

Another room is given over to knitting, and the girls pass from one type of work to another. We have a teacher from the Red Cross rooms who is showing the older girls how to make oakum pads. The work is really fascinating,

and fortunately we no longer have to think of the money
for the materials, as the work done in the schools has been
of so much higher standard that the local chapter has voted
me $500 in order that there might be no danger of our
stopping the work. I am inclosing a list of what our schools
have done in the past three months.

I. For the Red Cross Society
    1. Hospital Supplies
        Hospital boots   48
        Hospital shoulder wraps.   36
        Hospital shirts   156
        Pajama suits   48
        Surgeons' operating gowns.   6
        Surgeons' operating caps   12
        Surgeons' operating helmets   48
        Slings   492
        1-inch bandages   12
        2-inch bandages . . . .   13 rolls
    2. Surgical dressings   22
        Oakum pads   20
        Fracture pillows   20

II. For the Soldiers' Welfare League
    1. "Housewives" for Second New York Regiment   48
    2. "George Washington kits" for Second New York
        Regiment . . . .
    3. Neckerchiefs for Second New York Regiment .   120
    4. Pajama suits   32

III. For the National Navy Comforts League
    1. Knitted mufflers for the army and navy . . .   313
    2. Knitted sleeveless jackets for the army and navy .   25
    3. Knitted wristlets for the army and navy . . .   40 pairs
    4. Knitted caps for the army, navy, and aviators .   2
    5. Knitted hospital socks . . . .   7 pairs

IV. For the Surgical Dressings Committee (French)
   1. Slings
   2. Fracture pillows
   3. Eye binders

V. For Belgian Relief Committee
   1. Kits for small children (full set of clothes)

VI. For National League for Woman's Service (adults)
   1. Two commissariat classes
   2. Motor classes with 30 enrolled

Of course the Red Cross work need not be limited to girls and women. Boys under 14 are able to pick over oakum and to do other work that girls of the same age can do. The older boys can adjust and tend the knitting machines and pack and deliver the finished product.

Men and women in many of the state institutions will be glad to contribute a share in service. Thomas Mott Osborne, while warden at Sing Sing, organized through the Mutual Welfare League a large class of men who enthusiastically gave up their evening periods of recreation in order that they might knit for soldiers in foreign fields.

A number of young boys, none over 14, from Troy and Albany orphan asylums were taken in auto trucks 30 miles into the country to a currant-producing section, where they picked 5000 quarts of currants which had been donated to the county

Red Cross organization. These currants were shipped in a refrigerator car 90 miles down the river to Yonkers, New York, where the girls made them into jelly and currant juice, the sugar being donated by a local refinery.

Possibly the largest service that boys can render will be the making of Red Cross splints. As has already been stated in another chapter the Canadian schoolboys are doing a great deal of this work in connection with their manual training. An article in a recent issue of the *Manual Training Magazine* describes in detail the work of the manual-training centers of British Columbia. These splints are made merely for first aid, and are used where it is not necessary that they conform exactly to the contour of the limbs or body. They are padded a little with cotton or cloth and fitted on the injured part of the soldier.

A general conception prevails that Red Cross work is limited to battle-field relief, but it must be remembered that this organization also carries on civilian relief. It is very likely, as time goes on, that the schools will come to realize that there is probably no better agency than the Red Cross with which they can associate themselves in allaying the suffering and relieving the distress in the community. It must be remembered that the Red

Cross is splendidly organized, with its great central headquarters at Washington, its division head-quarters in larger groups of states, and its local chapters in every county. There is no activity of the Red Cross which a child cannot duplicate in its own sphere of life, and the American school may well become a center of interest in Red Cross work in time of war. One of the departments already organized is that of Home Service, which exists to help families maintain their standards of living. School-service work under a Junior Red Cross has been organized in order to bring the schools into direct touch with the work. The schools can give lessons in first aid, elementary hygiene, and home care of the sick, in home dietetics, and in the preparation of surgical dressings. It can make the necessary supplies for local soldiers who are in mobilization camps. It can make supplies for the soldiers' families, especially during the winter months. It can raise money by means of enter-tainments of an educational nature, and here op-portunities are often presented to correlate the work with history and English. In short, during the stress of war, with its rising cost of food, its industrial changes, its uncertainties in living con-ditions, with the home often handicapped by the withdrawal of the chief wage earner, there will be an excellent opportunity for the school to come in with its aid. The diet of the family, both in quality and variety, may be improved through the helpful advice of the teacher of home economics; children who are in need of medical care may be sent to the dispensary. The Home Service Department suggests that teachers may do helpful vocational-guidance work; for in the absence of father and older brothers many a boy and girl can be helped by a teacher's encouragement to go into occupations where there is a future, where skill can be acquired, and where there is a chance for advancement.

The following quotation from the London *Times* of some Red Cross work in France pointedly illustrates what home and school service in the Red Cross movement may mean in America.

The most detailed enumeration would hardly exhaust the activities of education in the common cause — voluntary contributions to the national funds deducted from the salaries of teachers; liberal subscriptions from pupils; participation in the collection of gold; the dispatch of packets to soldiers, and of books to the children of reconquered Alsace; help given to orphans whom a school or class has taken under its charge; manual labor on behalf of soldiers at the front, the wounded, the lame, and prisoners; material or moral assistance to refugees; a welcome given to all abandoned children, Belgian or French, in the families of masters or of friends of the school; correspondence with

Service recognizes no school grading. Girls of the lower grades are snipping waste pieces for fracture pillows and working with the older girls who are cutting hospital bed shirts, Troy, New York

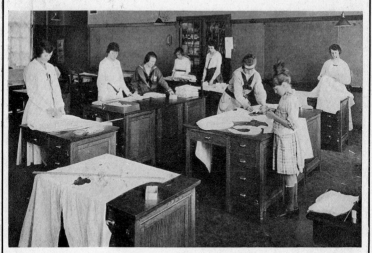

The new spirit of household arts in the schools is based upon the project plan and community service. War needs create new school practices. Troy (New York) girls at work on Red Cross supplies

A country school need not be idle during the summer. This one housed a group of farm cadets

Flying squadron leaving camp on an emergency call for berry pickers at Highland, New York

soldiers at the front, wounded, and prisoners ; attendance at
the funeral of soldiers who have died of their wounds ; the
public reception by schools, *lycées*, and universities of colleagues or old pupils wounded, promoted, or quoted in dis-
patches ; befriending soldiers who have no family to look
after them ; the institution of workrooms for men and women
who are out of work ; participation in the celebration of Belgian Day, the Serbian Day, the French Day, the Day of the
75, the Day of the Orphans, and so on, — tasks which will
have to be continued during the coming school year, because
the need for them will still be present, and doubtless, for
some of them at least, during the years immediately after
the war, when the school will still have before it a splendid
opportunity for social service.

President Wilson has honored the school children
of our country by a proclamation dated September
18, 1917, in which he calls upon them to do their
part in the war by joining the Junior Red Cross,
thus assisting in the mercy work of the senior
organization. A portion of his message is quoted :

The school is the natural center of your life. Through it
you can best work in the great cause of freedom to which
we have all pledged ourselves.

Our Junior Red Cross will bring to you opportunities of
service to your community and to other communities all
over the world, and guide your service with high and religious ideals. It will teach you how to save in order that
suffering children elsewhere may have the chance to live.
It will teach you how to prepare some of the supplies which

wounded soldiers and homeless families lack. It will send to you through the Red Cross bulletins the thrilling stories of relief and rescue. And, best of all, more perfectly than through any of your other school lessons, you will learn by doing those kind things under your teacher's direction to be the future good citizens of this great country which we all love.

Our President is a master of good pedagogy as well as a leader of men, and he expresses the very best in modern educational thought. He tells the children to think of their school as the natural center of their lives; to serve the community in which they live; to reach out through service and study to the larger world outside; to have behind all action high ideals; to save that others less fortunate may have; to learn how to do and through doing how to grow; to learn directly of the world of action while it is in action; to work with their elders for a common purpose, — the common purpose of being useful citizens of our great country.

CHAPTER IX

REËDUCATION OF THE DISABLED

In all probability not one person in a hundred ever heard the word "reëducation" before reading the very recent newspaper accounts of the government's plans as announced by Surgeon-general Gorgas for rehabilitating and reëducating the disabled soldiers. We have been in the habit of seeing blinded and crippled men selling lead pencils at street corners, and we have given our pity and our penny. We have seen the wonderful rugs woven by the blind (assisted in the designing and setting up by people who could see), and we have bought them, impelled by a sympathetic interest in a charitable cause. We have heard some exceptional person, who has overcome tremendous physical disabilities, describe her methods of studying college subjects and competing successfully with those who are unhandicapped, and we have said "How wonderful!" and stopped thinking at that point.

As a nation we have failed in our duty to make the physically handicapped economically self-supporting and normally strong. It is an educational problem as great as, if not greater than, that of assisting the mental defective.

Only within two years have the vocational schools of our country even thought of instructing their pupils in the general principles of safety. Only since workingmen's compensation laws and industrial insurance have come into the foreground in legislative halls have public men considered the appalling need for "safety-first" instruction in factories and in technical schools.

For the duration of the war our thought of safety appliances for industrial life in peaceful times sinks into the background, and we think only of devices for preventing suffocation by poisonous gases, of means of withstanding liquid fire, of deflectors for bullets and camouflage for marching troops. But notwithstanding all these precautions, the inevitable results of war are before us.

The multitude of men who have been injured in the present war is out of all proportion to the number injured in any war with which history or experience makes us acquainted, and the fitting of them to be economically self-supporting is a task of stupendous proportions. For the problem of the support of these men cannot be met entirely by pensions; even if this were possible, the man would thus become a dead weight for the rest of the country to carry, an unenviable position from all points of view. In the case of the professional man, he may, even if handicapped, carry on his work; but the man with a trade, when maimed or blinded, must be taught some other vocation or be provided with some mechanical substitute for his loss in legs or arms and often with special tools and other apparatus which will enable him to carry on his former occupation or a new one. It will not be possible to place all these men as ticket sellers, news vendors, gatemen, and in other positions hitherto appropriate for the industrially disabled; and our vocational schools, the medical profession, and the national government must coöperate in a study of the reëducation of injured soldiers with the aim of putting them on the pay roll.

On July 31, 1917, announcement was made through the press of the United States that a government system for the rehabilitation and reëducation of men disabled in the fighting abroad would be made an adjunct of the proposed scheme for the federal insurance of soldiers and sailors, and that the plans for the rehabilitation of these men would probably, like those in Canada, be modeled after the systems in use in France and England. It is, of course, part of the government's duty to provide for the future of men crippled in its service.

It is not the province of the several philanthropic
agencies which in the past have commendably
endeavored to care for the blind and the crippled
by teaching them the handiworks of weaving, brush-
making, etc. The work must be done on a sound
and scientific basis, and be adjusted to economic
conditions on a vast scale such as no philanthropic
society can hope to maintain; that is, it must not
be relief work, it must be governmental constructive work in reëducation which shall teach the disabled man how to overcome the disadvantage of
his infirmity in reëntering the industrial world.

To learn the extent of what may be done in this
work of rehabilitation, England, Canada, and the
United States look to France, — to the municipal
vocational-training school for soldiers at Lyons
known as L'École Joffre and the many schools
patterned after it in other cities; to the Institution
of St. Maurice, at Paris, which has been established by the French government to be a model
for other institutions; to the Laboratory of Research
on Vocational Work, in Paris, directed by Dr. Jules
Amar; and to the Anglo-Belgian hospitals, especially that at Vernon. It has been announced that the
United States will pattern its training school after
the Institution of St. Maurice, which is a clearing
house of experiments and research for the continent.

There are also in France, as in England and Canada, convalescent homes for disabled soldiers, — many of which are supported by private benevolence, — where trades are taught. At the Institute of Les Amis des Soldats Aveugles, in the suburbs of Paris, the blind soldiers are taught the trades of basket-making, bootmaking, brush-making, netting, harness-making, and bookbinding, the course taking about six months before the pupils become proficient. The institution runs its own printing establishment for literature in Braille (the print for the blind). The blind are peculiarly incapacitated, and the occupations open to them are consequently limited. Private benevolence has done much to lessen their economic misfortune, and the government must do more. Some French doctors believe that tobacco manufacturing and matchmaking are adapted to the blind because of their well-known delicacy of touch; many hospitals are giving them lessons in the art of massage, for the same reason, believing that the blind man can qualify for this employment in a few months. The work, however, is still in the experimental stage. But the most progressive work in France has been done in the municipal and government training schools in equipping the maimed and crippled for work, and it is this of which this chapter will treat.

The government institution of St. Maurice follows the lead of the now famous L'École Joffre, which in turn learned much from a school at Charleroi, maintained before the war for victims of industrial accidents. L'École Joffre was the pioneer which has blazed the way for the technical instruction of the wounded. It was founded under the direction of the city of Lyons, with the mayor of the city, Edouard Herriot, most active in the undertaking, and Maurice Barrès to spread its fame with winged words. To house it, an old disused château in a populous part of the city was put in order late in 1914, and early in 1915 the men discharged from the hospital and pronounced suitable for training entered upon their course of instruction. The first one hundred cases received were restricted to those disabled but cured of wounds, the partially paralyzed, and those recovered from amputation. To direct the technical work, Monsieur Basèque, a professor in the industrial-accident school at Charleroi, was chosen. The success of the school was immediate, and by September another was opened in the outskirts of the city to accommodate 80 men.

Naturally, at first, experiments were made, and the experience of L'École Joffre is most valuable to us. Three schemes were inaugurated: one, called *placement à domicile*, where an allowance was made the man, who was to live in his own home while he entered a workshop to learn a craft of some sort; another, *la mode de l'externat*, where the man pupil lived at his home or in lodgings while attending classes daily, receiving at the school at noon a canteen meal in order to save the time which would otherwise be taken in going home; and a third, *le régime de l'internat*, where he lived in the institution as a pupil in a boarding school. Experience developed that this last method was the only one which might be adopted with any assurance of success, the others subjecting the men to possible discouragement, through the jealousy shown by other shop workers, the necessarily slow progress, the inequality of pay, the varying degrees of instruction, and insufficient supervision. Canada too, after investigation, has found that the men throughout their training must live at the school and be under supervision, in order to avoid discouragement and the forming of bad habits of idleness and alcoholism, and to insure continuity of interest in their work.

The condition of entrance to L'École Joffre in Lyons is that the man must be pronounced permanently unfit for military service. Next he is examined to ascertain his fitness for industrial work, a matter determined by his freedom from disease, his previous work, his general education and ability, the employment preferred, and the occupations open. Whenever possible, the man is kept in his former employment. This principle is sound economically and psychologically, and must be adhered to in our schools. The employments for which training is given are bookkeeping, shorthand and typewriting, paper-stitching, bookbinding, toy-making, shoemaking, woodworking and drafting, tailoring, wood carving, gardening, and machine adjusting. Office work offers special opportunity to the one-handed and the crippled, as stenography and typewriting do to the blind. The course with commercial subjects, it was found, had to be carefully restricted, for many without sufficient education wished to take it up, and there was danger of sending too many men into occupations already well supplied with competent workers.

L'École Joffre is a municipal undertaking, a free school, the men pupils paying no board or tuition. It is in a measure subsidized, for the school receives from the Ministry of War a grant of 3 francs 50 centimes for each pupil for each day's attendance. The other funds to support the school are provided in various ways — popular subscriptions and grants by provincial organizations and other official bodies. As for the men themselves, they do not, while in training, receive the government pension of 1 franc 70 centimes a day, but the school makes each man an allowance of 1 franc 25 centimes a day from its own funds, so far as they permit of such liberality.

The work done by the city of Lyons has been followed in many localities, — Bourges, Bordeaux, Marseille, Rouen, and others, in most cases endowed by the municipalities. At Bourges additional classes are held in silver-engraving, hairdressing, and locksmith work.

In the similar school in Marseille, tinsmiths, foundry workers, jewelers, and metal workers are trained. At Cluses, in 1915, seventy partially disabled men were serving an apprenticeship in clock-making. This is sitting work, but it demands the possession of one hand and at least two fingers on the other, and an exceptionally good eye, so it is not so generally taught as other trades. At Cluny a course of training has been established for the former workmen who wish to become master workmen and designers; that is, the school specializes in training those whose ability is above the average.

It must be remembered that in French provinces there are many more hand processes in use than in the United States. Joinery and carpentry, for example, employ tools to make parts which in this country are turned out in factories. The industrial difference is evident in some of the photographs of the rehabilitated French workmen who are shown ingeniously at work with artificial " hands and arms " on processes for which there is no field here. Many French soldiers, too, find employment in toy making, a real industry for France and Germany, but one which is unlikely to be developed here to any extent. In America we must fit our disabled men to tend machines, and not make the blunder of preparing men for operations which are out of date in our standardized machine industries. In a very moving little book, " Les jeunes filles françaises et la guerre " (Jules Combarieu, Paris, 1916), we read of a man who was employed in a joinery establishment after suffering the amputation of both hands. His left arm was furnished with a leather glove to which was adapted an ingenious instrument for holding nails. His right · arm was fitted with another glove arrangement to which a hammer was attached. With the left he took the nails; and with the right he pounded them into a piece of wood. Marvelous as the achievement may be, in America this workman would belong to the class for whom special relief workshops must be maintained. Work in reëducation must naturally be adapted to the demands of the vicinity; the French towns of Nancy, Clermont, and Montpellier have not the industrial conditions of Pittsburgh, Worcester, or Birmingham.

In Paris the model government institution of St. Maurice contains both a convalescent hospital and a training school for discharged patients. It has the advantage over L'École Joffre of uniting hospital and school, giving an opportunity of combining physical with industrial reëducation. It is therefore possible to have at St. Maurice, under the direction of Dr. Bourillon, physiotherapy by massage, electricity, medical gymnastics, and mechanotherapy, which prepare the man for his reëducation. Dr. Bourillon affirms that this preliminary medical care reduces the effort which the patient must make to learn and exercise a trade.

The French government also maintains at Paris the Laboratoire des Recherches sur le Travail Professionel, — an establishment for the scientific examination of wounded men, particularly to ascertain the percentage of their disability in the labor market. The question of how many disabled men are capable of reëducation is one not rigidly determined. There are, of course, some hopeless cases which will have to be entirely dependent on the government for their support, whether by pension or other means under discussion. But the figures of Dr. Jules Amar, director of this laboratory of industrial research, a man who has devised mechanical apparatus for developing the capacities of injured limbs, show that of the maimed cases which have come under his observation at least 80 per cent are capable of vocational reëducation. Of this proportion 45 per cent succeed in earning normal salaries after a training including some specializing; 20 per cent are partially restored to normal wage earning; while the remaining 15 per cent can only obtain work in shops maintained especially for the disabled, such as a toymaking studio. Of the reëducation of this 80 per cent Dr. Amar says: "It is a question of science and method; it demands the organization of training schools. . . . It unites medical and technical knowledge to the end that artificial limbs shall be adapted to satisfy physical and vocational capabilities. The proportion of men dependent upon relief is then reduced; and one must endeavor, without ceasing, to diminish it."[1]

The method in the Paris schools is scientific. "In the training schools," he continues, "the object

[1] Special Bulletin of Military Hospitals Commission, Canada, April, 1916.

of the instruction is to supplement the diminished physical capacity of the disabled man with a greater knowledge of his trade, superior technical instruction, or better vocational adjustment."

The first responsibility falls on the medical examiner. To reëquip the maimed physically, an indispensable prosthesis (an addition of an artificial part to supply the missing member of the body) is made, the *dynamical* prosthesis — not the kind which *replaces* the member, but that which reëstablishes or repairs the *functions*. What the wounded man needs is not an admirable imitation of the missing arm or leg, ingenious and often fragile appliances, but a practical working tool, — a socket into which a variety of tools can be fitted.

Next, in the laboratory of the school an analysis of the workman's movements is made in relation to their regularity, direction, speed, and according to the force they expend. The measure of the man's physical incapacity is deduced from impressions gathered in this analysis, and from it the method of training must be devised. Furnished with his card of qualifications, the man passes from the hospital laboratory to the workshop, where experts instruct him in theory and practice. The first thing to determine is whether a man cannot perform the operations of his former trade. In many

cases a man imagines that the disability caused by
amputation of fingers, hand, or arm makes him
unfit for the work he did previous to the war.
But where the school is attached to a hospital
and the man's disability can be accurately known,
the union of medical skill and technical instruction makes it possible to restore him to usefulness with the minimum of effort and waste.

Dr. Amar recommends for special relief work
for the 15 per cent who are not capable of any
great degree of reëducation, shops which will exe-
cute orders for easily manufactured articles, involving such processes as light cooperage, stamping,
plaiting, toymaking,—work such as is offered at
the shop in Rue de la Durance, Paris.

Another institution whose methods are similar
to those employed at St. Maurice and by Dr. Amar
is the Anglo-Belgian Military Institute, at Port
Villez, Vernon, under the technical director Major
Haccourt. It accommodates over 800 men, and is
self-supporting, the land where it is situated having been originally covered with forests, the sale
of which financed the undertaking at first. Forty-
three trades are taught here, and a large farm is
maintained on which horses wounded in war are
cared for and made useful. The workshops provide for commercial courses, telegraphy, wall-paper

designing, the manufacture of motor vehicles and electrical machinery of all kinds, plumbing and tinsmithing, rabbit and poultry farming, fur curing and dyeing, etc. The shops make fuse boxes for munitions, and various army supplies. At Vernon the men pupils are regarded as still in the Belgian army, receiving military pay; they have no option as to entrance, since they are under military discipline, but enter as soon as they are discharged from the Anglo-Belgian hospital at Rouen. In this school the services of the best professors in different trades are obtained without trouble, for the director can requisition any man in the Belgian army for any required purpose. Before the war Belgium had a large proportion of highly trained workmen; and with compulsory reëducation and military discipline the operation of this institution is much simplified.

In working out plans for reëducation in the United States we must have in mind certain principles. There is the necessity of making our training thorough. Our problem will be not to find employment for the period of the war, during which there is a constant demand for workers, but to train the disabled for an occupation in which they can hold a place after the temporary shortage of labor created by the war conditions is over. It is obvious that if the men are incompetent and ill-prepared for their work, they will be weeded out as soon as skilled men are available. Their work is barred from that demanding manual strength; nor can it hope to belong to that highly specialized kind which would demand an arduous and elaborate training. But there is a wide range of semiskilled occupations where a handicapped man can earn more than if he should enter after a long course of training the highly skilled trade where he would meet the competition of the physically normal.

There are at least three kinds of disabilities our schools will have to deal with. First, there is the man who has lost his right arm. This man must, whenever possible, be taught to use his left hand in his trade, although it is sometimes easier to learn a new process than to change right-hand to left-hand methods in the old operation. In carpentry, turning, and machine trades, however, the one-armed man may continue to be employed, and our vocational schools should incorporate courses in left-hand training. Here also we find another need: there must be built for the disabled *left-hand machines*.

Next there is the case of the man who must be instructed in an allied trade because his former one is pronounced by medical examination and the tests of mechanotherapy to be impossible. And last there is the case of the man whose injury makes necessary the fitting of delicately adjusted prosthesis and a course of expert training before he can become a wage earner.

Our chief difficulty in our work of reëducation will be to secure the right kind of teaching force, and it is clear that our government must establish schools to train our technical instructors how to adapt their knowledge of trade teaching to the kind of work demanded in giving instruction to the physically disabled. The selection of the proper type of teacher is vital to the success of any scheme of reëducation. The ideal instructor must not only know his trade but be able to suit his methods to the individual case so as to get the best response from each man under his direction. At present it seems as if there would be no way of training instructors except by sending chosen trade teachers to St. Maurice to study the French methods, that they may return to this country properly equipped to select and instruct others, until such time as a government school of the right type is well established in this country.

As for the schools themselves, they must be undertaken by the government, even if additional hospitals and laboratories for research are maintained by private benevolence and bequest, for there should be no limit to the funds available for carrying on this work of the economic rehabilitation of the men injured in the service of the country, and it must keep pace with the progressive work in France and elsewhere. Branch schools in municipalities may be organized under government control and subsidized by federal money. Some of our trade and vocational schools and their equipment may be taken over by the government for this purpose. Our trade and technical schools must also include courses in training teachers for this special work, the course to be supplemented by a special preparation prescribed by the government.

In Canada the Military Hospitals Commission has made a careful study of the French and Anglo-Belgian treatment in the restoration of disabled soldiers, and has equipped the Central Military Convalescent Hospital at Toronto with the mechano-apparatus similar to that used in France by Dr. Amar and Dr. Bourillon. Profiting by their observation of the foreign hospital schools, they have determined to consider the men in training as still in hospital and under military rule, for in Europe there is absolute unanimity of opinion that the influence of convalescent homes and benevolent support is bad, conducive to lax discipline and idleness. Canada has agreed that the earning power subsequently acquired by a pensioner in training will not lessen his pension. To pass upon the cases eligible for reëducation, Canada has a board of three: a member of the Provincial Advisory Committee, a vocational officer, and a medical man, thus combining with technical and medical aid advice in the industrial choice and placement of the man pupil.

Realizing that reëducation is a new idea to most soldiers and, indeed, to the public generally, Canada has put forth a propaganda of making popular the training courses. A bulletin has been posted conspicuously in public buildings and a printed card circulated bearing the same information, " What Every Disabled Soldier Should Know." Aside from encouragement and directions of where to obtain help, etc., we find the following:

That his strength and earning capacity will be restored in the highest degree possible.

That if his disability prevents him from returning to his old work, he will receive free training for a new occupation.

That full consideration is given to his own capacity and desires when a new occupation has to be chosen.

That neither his treatment nor his training nor his transportation will cost him a cent.

That his maintenance and his family's will be paid for during his training and for a month after.

That his home province has a special commission to assist him in finding employment on discharge.

To further the publicity of the work in Canada, moving-picture films have been prepared, systematically illustrating the treatment and reëducation of wounded soldiers in England, France, and Canada, and showing their progress up to the stage of final recovery. These films have been shown in hundreds of theaters throughout the Dominion.

It is encouraging that occasionally in France and Canada the vocational training in connection with hospitals places a man in a better position financially than before. The following examples are given out by the Canadian Military Hospitals Commission and are testimonials of the possibilities of rehabilitation.

Letter received is from an ex-private in the 13th Battalion. Before enlistment he was getting $12 a week as driver on a city milk round. "I always had a liking for drawing," he says, "and I felt that if I ever had the chance I would take up a course in mechanical drawing." This opportunity came to him at one of the commission's convalescent hospitals. After six weeks' application to the work there, he was able to secure an appointment beginning with $75 a month, with good prospects of advance.

A locomotive fireman had enlisted, was severely wounded, and had to have his left arm amputated. Under the commission's scheme of reëducation, which is offered to all men incapacitated for their former work by service, he received special training in telegraphy and railway routine. As a result he secured an appointment as station agent and dispatcher at $110 a month.

In England the high sheriff of Lancashire has formulated a scheme for listing the employments open to the disabled. First, the employer is asked, whenever possible, to give the returned soldier his old job. Next, certain employments are listed as being within the powers of partially disabled men, and with the help of labor exchanges and of other agencies, these are reserved for them.

It is for the economic interest of the State to make possible the employment of the disabled. The amount of a pension is not the measure of the cost of the pensioner. The nation cannot afford to let any human power go to waste or lie idle. To reëquip the maimed is to make him partly forget his infirmity, — an indispensable mental advantage. France is now discussing whether reëducation of one form or another shall be compulsory, as in the Anglo-Belgian hospital. "But obligatory or not," says A. L. Bittard,[1] "the industrial reëducation must be above all a national work. We should regard it as a debt owed to the wounded and as an effective preparation for the future of the nation. . . . The State alone is capable of giving all the mutilated the maximum equality of treatment, where private initiative would be totally incapable of realizing the minimum."

[1] A. L. Bittard, Les Écoles de Blessés. Paris, 1916.

The war simply makes the question of reëducating and rehabilitating the disabled a striking one. But we must not forget that the problem of the injured is always with us. It may not be amiss to point out that 54,001 men and women were actually killed in the United States during the year 1913. This means one killed every ten minutes. Over 2,000,000 men and women are injured in the industries in the United States each year. This means one injured every sixteen seconds. The economic loss from accidental deaths and injuries is nearly $500,000,000 annually, and the loss from preventable accidents and diseases would more than pay the cost of maintaining all the public schools in the United States. These are appalling figures.

At present the great fear of every boy who goes to war and of every sister and mother of such a boy is that he may go through life maimed and dependent. But we never think of the ever-present danger to these boys of being handicapped physically by merely going to work; and yet there are more persons so disabled through accidents in industrial life in normal times than are disabled by war.

When our boys come back from the war, physically disabled, and through the government work in rehabilitation and reëducation are made self-supporting and self-respecting members of society,

we shall begin to appreciate that we have been extremely negligent in the past in limiting our efforts
to help the crippled and blinded to the good offices
of charity and philanthropy.   It is a public matter.
It is a problem of education.   It is an opportunity
for service for the teachers of vocational training,
for the experts in vocational guidance and direction, for the directors of placement and employment
bureaus, and for the designers of special tools and
machines for the handicapped.   It is an immediate problem in this time of war; it is even more
significant in time of peace.

CHAPTER X

FARM CADETS

We can afford only one fad in war time, and that fad is to be farming. It will be useless for little William Corning Smith, aged 12, of Kankakee, Illinois, to stick his little spade into his back yard before his admiring parent. Individual, unorganized work on land not properly prepared for agriculture may be worse than useless; it may be wasteful. Random efforts not coördinated in a general scheme for the utilization of school children in large units will be foolish, misdirected effort. State, county, and even national organization are required to make available this latent power. Purely isolated effort will be fruitless, both as aids to the nation and education for the child. Organized work will bring the greater moral advantages of developing the power of concentration along with the interest in national and community service. It will evoke an esprit de corps. which may be capitalized for national use and shift the usual interest in gangs and athletics, both normal and natural, to work which opens the way to loyal industrial educational training.[1]

This was written by John Dewey early in the spring of 1917 in a message addressed to the principals and teachers of America on how school children may be so organized for farm service as to

[1] Columbia University War Papers.

Aid the nation;

Increase the food supply of the country in war time and during a world-wide shortage of food;

Conscript the national enthusiasm for athletics to national usefulness;

Assure a vigorous and healthy rising generation;

Reap the advantage of organized effort with its moral and educational results;

Develop constructive patriotism.

As may be gathered, Dewey's idea was not only to organize the rural and village children for farm work but also to send the city children into the country in camps and tent colonies. He said further that the plan was not a dream and that it could be done.

A friend in writing to me of his attempts in Massachusetts to make the dream a reality said, " It is like nailing a jellyfish to a board." Referring to the difficulty of obtaining competent boys, on the one hand, and of convincing farmers of the value of city-boy labor, on the other, he further stated that it was a difficult proposition to sell something we did not have to somebody who did not want it.

Few, if any, of us knew very much of the experience, in this direction, of England, France, and Germany. To be sure, we had heard that France had attempted in a large way to use children at farm labor, but had given it up and had replaced them with old men, women, and partially crippled returned soldiers; and we knew that with the alarm of the scarcity of labor and the diminishing number of the world's acres under cultivation England and Germany had called upon women and boys below military age to help meet the needs of the situation. But we in America did not realize, to quote Dewey again, " that we could enlist the school children in this work in such a manner that they could serve with results as beneficial to themselves as to the nation."

Before considering in some detail the idea of using agricultural labor of children in America (and it is a subject worthy of elaboration, for even if the war closes to-morrow, we shall be short of farm labor for many years — perhaps always), let us see what England and Germany have done to utilize school children for farm work.

In England many of the boys of 14 to 16 in the public schools have volunteered for vacation and holiday agricultural work in hoeing, planting, and harvesting; some of this was gratuitous labor, these boys coming from the prosperous classes and therefore being able to give their services.

In July, 1916, the Education Board published a report showing the number of children excused from attendance at school for the purpose of agricultural employment in England and Wales on May 31, 1916. The total number so excused was 15,753, of which number 546 were between the ages of 11 and 12; 8018 between 12 and 13; 5521 between 13 and 14, and of the remaining 1668 cases the ages were between 12 and 14. Figures quoted relate solely to agricultural employment and do not show the full extent of withdrawals from school. They also relate to withdrawals of children who are not qualified for total exemption under the law. The report also states that "the board has no information as to the number of children who have been excused from school attendance for purposes of industrial employment or employment other than agriculture."

Early in 1917 several of the county education committees formulated plans for using the labor of children who were to be excused only for holidays, special periods, and part times, the general sentiment being, even in the emergency, that no more children must be permanently excused for agricultural or industrial employment. These schemes are worthy of attention as endeavors to retain children in school, at the same time modifying the arrangement of the educational requirements to allow them to perform farm and garden work.

The Education Committee for the Lindsay division of Lincolnshire considered, at a meeting held on April 13, 1917, the desirability of taking steps to secure that the school holidays this year are fixed at such times as will enable the children to be of most assistance to the farmers, and it was resolved that the finance committee should be requested to consider the preparation of a scheme enabling managers to amend the school time-tables in such a way as will give the maximum of opportunity for the older children to work on the land during the spring and summer. . . . They further considered . . . that in view of the present emergency and the need of additional labor, especially in agricultural work, the board will give favorable considerations to proposals for extended or additional holidays in rural areas under certain conditions. Two schemes were presented, setting forth alternative methods which managers might be authorized to adopt by which advantage can be taken of the concessions of the board, as follows : (1) A scheme to give a number up to eighty additional afternoons on which the older children can be employed on the land, managers to be informed that a school year of not less than 320 attendances will be accepted as fulfilling the requirements of the board, instead of a minimum of 400 as heretofore. On up to eighty days, older children, above prescribed age, may be released at noon for employment on the land, whilst the school will be open as usual for the younger children, and their attendance recorded, though not in the official register. (2) A scheme to allow up to eight weeks extra during which the older children may be employed on the land, managers to be informed of the number of attendances required as in scheme one. Older children, above a prescribed age, who are to be employed on the land, need not attend school for a period up to eight weeks in addition to the ordinary holidays. The school will be kept open as usual during such weeks for the younger children, and those attending will have their attendance recorded, but not in the official register. Under either scheme it will be necessary for the managers to fix the period or periods for the year during which the scheme would be in operation, and in some of the larger rural schools it might be possible to release a teacher as well as the older children.

At a meeting held on April 27 it was resolved to issue the schemes to the managers, impressing upon them the fact that the one object is to secure increased production of food.[1]

At Grimsby a committee was appointed to consider the employment of children on gardens, allowing an acre plot to each school, and 25 children, under a teacher, to work in cultivating it. All these children are required to attend school in the morning, and the consent of their parents must be obtained by them before they are permitted to begin afternoon work. Since, as in Lincolnshire, the aim of the work is increased food production, the crops derived from the cultivation of the land acquired by the town are to be divided among teachers and scholars engaged in the work.

In Hull, also, the Educational Committee, besides encouraging work in school gardens, has authorized

[1] London *Times*, Educational Supplement, May 17, 1917.

the labor of schoolboys in cultivating spare land in various places as a substitute for their usual manual training in the school shops.

In Hertfordshire there are school gardens for the production of potatoes, parsnips, beets, and onions, with school instruction in gardening given the pupils. During the period for planting there is a schedule of half-time attendance. In Bradford the successful vegetable gardening is correlated with the school work in nature study, composition, arithmetic, and drawing, and emphasis is placed on the educational value of the productive work.

It is difficult for America to see the food crisis as do the nations which are near the exhaustion point. While everyone must deplore the wholesale excusing of children to work without supervision, we ought to watch with interest all schemes which will increase production and yet will keep younger children in school for full time and will permit those older to work part time. This part-time work should be confined to the years of 14 to 18, except possibly in the case of work in the school garden, where younger children may labor for short periods.

The appeal of Neville Chamberlain, the Director-general of National Service, in the spring of 1917, for volunteers from such boys as were able to make the sacrifice, connects the need for agricultural

labor with the necessity for providing proper supervision of the boys. His plan for utilizing the labor
of English schoolboys has many features similar to
devices employed in Massachusetts, New York, and
New Jersey.

It is well understood that an abundant supply of labor
for the land during the coming summer months is an urgent
national necessity. Many schemes have already been organized for the employment of soldiers, women, and prisoners
of war, but it is desirable to form a reserve of labor so
organized as to be available at short notice. For this
reserve I turn to the boys at our public and other secondary
schools. During the last two years many of them have
given valuable help in hoeing, harvesting, and timber cutting, and at the present crisis I confidently hope that all
for whom it is possible will make their services available
both in summer holidays and, if necessary, during the
coming term. I have accepted the offer of the Cavendish
Association to place at my disposal their organization,
which will act in conjunction with a committee — representative of schools and masters — having its headquarters
at St. Ermin's, and working under the director of the agricultural section of this department. Full particulars of the
arrangements and procedure will shortly be issued by the
committee. The main points are as follows :

(1) The age of the boys permitted to volunteer should
not be below 16 except in the cases where the school
authorities consider boys of 15 sufficiently strong to undertake the necessary work. (2) The boys will be organized in
squads of varying sizes, each in charge of a master or other

responsible person. (3) It is proposed that during term time the period of continuous whole-time service should not exceed two weeks. Every effort will be made to find work for schoolboy volunteers in the neighborhood of the school, but if the work lies at some distance from the school, railway fares will be paid and careful provision will be made for board and lodging. No boy will be expected to volunteer for service during term whose school work is of immediate importance; for example, a boy who is preparing for a scholarship examination. I recognize that this part of the scheme may present some difficulties to all but the large public schools, but I hope that some of the larger state-aided secondary schools may be able to join in it. Before doing so, however, they should communicate with the Board of Education. (4) In the holidays they will work for not less than three or four weeks, and it is hoped that, if necessary, they may have leave of absence from school until the end of September. (5) The whole working hours will be carefully proportioned to the average strength of each squad, and the wages adjusted accordingly. If the total sum earned does not meet the cost of living, the deficit will under special conditions be made up.

I trust that when the call for boys' help comes, parents will recognize its urgency and will not hesitate to allow their sons to render this service for their country.

In Germany there has been a systematic contribution from schools to agriculture since March, 1915. Authority was given to the respective school officials to grant the necessary leave of absence to older children for farm and garden cultivation.

With the increasing need of securing a sufficient supply of food for the nation, excuses of pupils from school increased. An additional service of pupils was required by an order issued on May 15, 1917, relative to combating fruit and vegetable pests.

Looking forward to future scarcity, Germany, with the help of the teaching staff and government leaflets, next enlisted school children in the work of collecting field and forest edible products. Children were engaged in the work of gleaning, and in the summer of 1915 the gleanings amounted to approximately $50,000, the greater part of which was turned over to the Red Cross as the children's contribution. In the summer and autumn of 1915 the children aided, too, in gathering fruits. During the following winter the schools gave instruction in the substitution of fruit products for fat and proteid. These were pointed lessons both in frugality and in public spirit.

Additional requirement of the children's services was made when the continued scarcity of fats made it imperative to conserve acorns, horse-chestnuts, and seeds containing oil, the gathering of which was impossible without the aid of school children. An order of August 21, 1916, authorized the employment of children to take part in the extraction from trees in the state forests of resin needed chiefly for the paper industry; and in the same season children were called upon to engage in the collection of kernels of cherries, plums, and apricots in enormous quantities for oil extraction.

The school administrators and teachers of America knew little, if anything, of the farm-placement ventures of European countries. But they were told most emphatically in the spring of 1917 that the military force was but one factor in national organization, and that the ultimate decision as to victory might well be with the farmer. So in American fashion we started at it; New Jersey with its "junior industrial army," Massachusetts with its bronze-badged boy farmers, and New York with its "farm cadets."

We all thought we were original, and perhaps we were; and yet it is certainly not new for school-boys to work outside the school session when of proper age. Whether for the father or a neighborhood employer, boys 14 and over have worked in stores and gardens, in summer hotels, in offices, garages, and manufacturing plants. Nor is it unusual, for that matter, to have the outside work coördinated with the school and receiving due credit in the curriculum. The coöperative high-school and vocational courses in many cities — Fitchburg, Beverly, Providence, Hartford, Indianapolis, Chicago, and New York — are well known to those who are familiar with the extension and coöperative efforts of our vocational schools.

Furthermore we are familiar with the two types of camps: the adult-labor and the recreation camp. The work camp is much the older, dating back to the building of railroads and the opening of lumber districts. In the past decade the recreation summer camps have become a potent factor in secondary-school life, making a complement of the school year's work by laying stress on the physical development of outdoor woodland and country experiences. Some of these camps, while primarily recreational, have had courses in manual training, college preparation, arts and crafts, and languages, yet so clearly is their play nature of chief importance that no one thinks of them as work camps.

Now the farm-cadet movement involves the farm labor of the schoolboy, who is sent out and credited for his work by his school and is added to a camp life where in a squad of his fellow schoolboys he is looked after by an appointed leader as if in a Y.M.C.A. camp. Thus we have, out of familiar ingredients, a new compound, bringing into relation the boy, the parent, the supervisor, the employer, and the school.

This agricultural movement in connection with the schools had its inception at the Philadelphia meeting of the Eastern Arts and Manual Training Teachers' Association early in 1917. At once three Eastern states — Massachusetts, New Jersey, and New York — began to formulate plans for its operation.[1] For it was not to be the simple expedient of excusing boys from school to work on farms, as has been the practice in many localities, but a plan whereby the boy was to be retained in the school system, substituting in his course during a portion of the year agricultural work for the academic and vocational studies of the regular curriculum.

In analyzing the problem it was found that there were three types of boys to be considered: (1) the boy in a farming district, who could be employed on the farm of his father or a neighbor; (2) the boy in a town near an agricultural center, who could be employed within a radius of a few miles of his home and school; (3) the boy from a city, who would have to be sent to distant farms and whose welfare would not be in the charge of his school principal and parents. The case of the first boy is very simple; the second is also easy of solution; but if the third boy is to be used,

---

[1] California and Indiana developed plans about the same time. Before the first of July, 1917, the movement became quite general in America.

there will need to be a carefully worked-out plan for his placement, record of work, accommodations, and general welfare. It is for the third boy that the camp must be established, where he will be looked after by a responsible person who will see that he has the proper tent, board, work, and sanitary arrangements.

The plans of the different states for utilizing boy power, while aiming toward the one desirable end of increasing our food production, have differed widely in detail, owing to the variation in the compulsory-attendance laws, to the latitude exercised in some states in excusing boys prematurely, and to the varying degrees of investigation of placement, record of work, and supervision. All states agree in giving the boy who is excused for farm work credit in his school work. Canada, too, excuses boys over 14 for farm work, allowing them full school credit for three months' labor. While it may be urged that it is not pedagogically sound to give credit in one subject for the work in another, a way out of the difficulty might be found in a rearrangement of the school year and vacations in districts where there is a large percentage of excused boys; or special classes could be devised for these boys when they return to school. In the large high schools shorter intensive

courses could be included in the program so that
the boy who was preparing for college would not
lose his work in such subjects as English, history,
and mathematics. In the case of language and
science there must be a loss which it is difficult
to repair. If the present conditions persist, administrative ingenuity can solve the question of work
and credits. It is not one of the serious aspects of
the problem, provided always that there is no release
of children below the compulsory-attendance age.

In Massachusetts the work of mobilizing schoolboys for farm labor was in charge of the state's
Committee on Public Safety. Their principles in
acting were as follows:

Mobilize the schoolboys; keep those under 16 at home to
work on home, school, and community gardens; enlist the
high-school boys between 16 and 18, too young for military
or naval service, but old enough to render real service; move
them where farm labor is needed; make them understand
that enlistment for farm service is in all ways as patriotic
as any other service for the nation's defense.

With the appointment of a subcommittee to formulate the detailed scheme of placement and supervision, having Frank V. Thompson, Assistant
Superintendent of the Boston schools, as chairman, the plan for the coöperation of schools with
agriculture is, for boys 16 and over, as follows:

1. (*a*) The farm-labor service is to be recognized by a bronze badge containing the seal of the commonwealth and inscribed " The Nation's Service " and " Food Production." (*b*) An honorable discharge, similar to a discharge from the army, containing the signature of the governor, will be issued to boys who successfully complete their service on farms. (*c*) Tufts, Boston University, Massachusetts Institute of Technology, and Massachusetts Agricultural College have agreed to give a trial term or year to such candidates as present an honorable discharge, without further entrance requirements, provided their school work was satisfactory up to the time of leaving and the principal so recommends.

2. The existing school organization is used to conduct the enterprise. For each 25 boys enlisted a supervisor is appointed, a male teacher of strong ability in the local school,—in towns where there are several supervisors, either the superintendent of schools or the principal of the high school. A general head supervisor in charge of the state work has an office in the Statehouse. Each local head supervisor and each supervisor of 25 boys receives the same sum ($100), the money being obtained from a local contingent fund, from an additional appropriation, or by subscription.

3. The minimum wage of the boys is fixed thus:

first week, no wages, but allowance of $2 for expenses etc.; thereafter (a) boy living on farm, not less than $4 a week and board, (b) boy living at home, not less than $6 a week. Six days constitute a week.

4. The enlistment card and the issuance of honorable discharge are controlled by the general head supervisor (Committee on Public Safety).

5. The enrollment for the period of May 1 to October 1 is made by the boy, with the parents' consent and the school physician's indorsement. When the boy is enlisted, a numbered badge is lent to him, for which he signs a receipt; it is to be returned in case of unsatisfactory conduct or service. He receives full credit for the year's school work.

6. Inspection of the physical and moral conditions of the place of employment, the choosing of the boys from enrollment lists, and seeing that both boys and farmers are satisfied, are part of the work of the appointed supervisors.

7. Camps for the boys, when local conditions require, are established under the direction of the medical expert for the State Board of Labor and Industries. An expert on camps has supervision of the work of the executive committee in standardizing and inspecting camps and obtaining the equipment, layout, and food supplies.

With the coöperation of farm bureaus thousands of circulars and labor-contract forms were sent to Massachusetts farmers. By June 16, 1917, there were camps established at 18 points, and arrangements completed to employ 500 to 600 boys from these camps. In addition there were at least 500 other boys released from school to work on home farms, or living in farmers' homes.

An interesting feature of the Massachusetts scheme was the working out of camp plans by the drafting students in the Newton Technical High School, with detailed equipment of dining tent with wooden-horse tables; sleeping tent with double-deck bunk; latrine; cook shack; etc.

In its system for handling the supply of boy labor, the state requires the farmer to sign a definite application blank for the amount of boy labor which he requires. It is understood that while the boys are enlisted for the entire period up to October 1, the farmer may take those boys for long or short periods of not less than a week in duration, to begin or end at any time, as the farmer's necessity requires. This application made by the farmer is also an agreement to pay the wages stipulated by the Committee on Public Safety and also to employ the boy on rainy as well as fair days, using his services on rainy days under cover if possible. Further agreement is made, in case the boy is unsatisfactory, to give him one week's notice or one week's pay, providing him with a statement in writing of the reason for his discharge. Whenever, in the opinion of the local supervisor, the conditions of living or of labor are not satisfactory, the boy may be withdrawn without prejudice to him. These arrangements insure that there shall be a coöperative responsibility of farmer and state in caring for the boy.

In establishing the camps in Massachusetts the money to start the work was chiefly supplied by individuals. In the case of the New Bedford contingent in Coonamesett camp, on an estate of 11,000 acres, the boys were housed in militia tents, lent by the state, — two boys to a tent. For their tent furnishings the boys supplied whatever they needed. A mess house — a rough board building 75 feet long by 17 feet wide, providing eating quarters for the boys and at one end a cook room — was in part erected by the New Bedford Industrial School boys, working under the direction of an experienced carpenter. The laying of the 2500 feet of pipe to carry water to the camp was also the work of the same school. The catering for the boys was under the direction of an experienced woman and two Japanese cooks. In the morning the boys started for the various farms, those at a distance being called for by an auto truck. In this camp, for an eight-hour day and a six-day week each boy received a maximum wage of $4 a week and board, the weekly payment in charge of the supervisor. The camp was fortunate in having as its directors the city superintendent of schools and a physical instructor, the latter living in the camp.

In New York the placing of boys on farms has been the joint work of the Food Supply Commission, the State Education Department, and the State Military Training Commission. While younger boys have been released for agricultural work by other agencies, the state placement by the commission is concerned only with the boys of military training age — 16 to 19. One of the first actions of the latter commission was to divide the state into 6 military-training zones: New York City (including Manhattan, Bronx, and Richmond); Long Island, including Brooklyn; Hudson Valley, with center at Albany; East Central, at Syracuse; West Central, at Rochester; and Western, at Buffalo. Next, a description was obtained of the character of the work in each zone. For example, the Hudson Valley Zone as far as Albany requires labor in harvesting small fruits and general farm work, while the West Central Zone work is that of muck farming, large-fruit farming, and general farming. Each zone center has its individual office through which placements are made. Meetings were held the latter part of April by zone supervisors and farm-bureau managers, and attended by farmers' and fruit growers' associations who stated what they needed and what they would contribute in wages and housing for boy workers.

The inducements for enlisting offered by the state to boys released from school work were the chevron given by the Military Training Commission, to be awarded after thirty days' satisfactory work; the military-training-equivalent value of the service; and the promise of proper pay and care by the employer. As to credits, so important in the New York system, farm cadets were permitted to take the Regents' examinations though the course lacked a few weeks of completion, the time requirement being waived in their case. Any pupil in the schools of the state who enlisted for military service (this applied to the colleges) or who rendered satisfactory agricultural service was credited with the work of the term without examination, on the certificate of the school that his work up to the time of enlistment was satisfactory.

New York is an agricultural state, with a great variety of kinds of farming and many districts remote from centers of the supply of labor. The agricultural census, to which reference was made in Chapter II, supplied data for determining the districts where and when labor was most needed and where schoolboys could be most useful. For example, in Orleans County, in the Western Zone, the demand varied from 163 laborers needed early in May to 1521 needed in October, an indication that there was really more reason for excusing boys in October than in May for work in peach- and apple-harvesting districts.[1] Conspicuous among the types of New York farms where labor was sought were the great fruit farms, such as the Sodus Fruit Farm, with a house on the shore of Lake Ontario able to accommodate 100 boys, where it was planned to harvest the entire peach and apple crop with schoolboy labor; the vast tracts owned by the canning companies, with thousands of acres of

---

[1] The following statistics for Orleans County show how agricultural help is needed, as indicated by the census taken by school children:

May 10–20	163	Aug. 21–31	573
May 21–31	165	Sept. 1–10	1157
June 1–10	227	Sept. 11–20	1308
June 11–20	257	Sept. 21–30	1317
June 21–30	271	Oct. 1–10	1521
July 1–10	518	Oct. 11–20	1500
July 11–20	526	Oct. 21–30	1435
July 21–31	523	Nov. 1–10	38
Aug. 1–10	486	Nov. 11–20	13
Aug. 11–20	554	Nov. 20–30	1

tomatoes, beans, and corn under cultivation; and the farms such as those in the South Lima district, where there was muck farming and where the work included the cultivating, sorting, and packing of onions, lettuce, celery, and spinach. Calls were sometimes made upon the state for as many as 1500 boys to assist in harvesting. It was therefore necessary for the state to work on a large and definitely planned scale.

Naturally the first boys to be placed were those residing in or near farming districts. When, however, the supply of these boys was exhausted, the call came, even from remote districts, for city boys. In these cases the problem of transportation becomes serious, as well as the housing and care of the boy in the new environment, where association with other help is apt to be harmful.

The following description of a New York State camp is offered not only because it has proved to be highly successful but also because it affords an excellent illustration of the "farm-working, or labor-distributing, camp," which is defined in the chapter following.

It was called The Erasmus Hall High School (New York City) Potato Growers' Association, and was organized by F. A. Rexford, a teacher who is much interested in agriculture and in boys.

Working and living in the berry fields. One of twenty-five camps in the Highlands of New York State

Agriculture on a Western basis brings lessons in organization, coöperation, and economy to Eastern boys. City boys working on a large farm near Phoenixville, Pennsylvania

Employing able-bodied boys of city high schools for farm production may become permanent. It may lead to the development of country annexes to our city schools. Camp near Phoenixville, Pennsylvania

The object of the association, which was formed in the school, was originally fourfold: (1) to teach the farmer that the alert city boy can and will perform agricultural tasks; (2) to increase the food supply; (3) to relieve the help situation by organizing a group of boys to work by the hour or day, and to recruit boys to work by the month for individual farmers under supervision; (4) to fit boys for military service if needed.

Ten boys from the school left New York on May 5, each armed with the money necessary to pay such expenses as carfare, food, laundry, rent of an acre of land, seed potatoes, phosphate, team hire, and spraying materials. They went to Mr. Rexford's farm, located up-state. The *New York Tribune* contributed some money, and one of the teachers in the school advanced $60 for the boys to grow potatoes for him. Some frail boys, whose parents wanted them to go for their health, were refused.

At first the farmers were skeptical. The boys, however, went to work on the land which they had rented from Rexford. In a week they began to attract attention and farmers began to hire them. Rexford knew some of these farmers by reputation. He believed that men who cannot keep their own boys at home cannot succeed with boys from the city. He was in the habit of having a straight talk with the employing farmers, telling them that the boys must be treated squarely.

A large milk-distributing corporation offered to take every one of his boys, but he argued that it could afford to hire men and did not need boys, as did the farmers who could not obtain other help. It is evident that large farmers have capital and backing, while it is the individual farmer struggling with hard conditions who must have help.

Most of the boys who are with farmers by the month come back to the main camp every Sunday morning for physical examination, general assembly, and to go to church. This coming back to the camp keeps before them the idea of a camp for farm cadets. They return to their work Sunday night. For those boys who go out by the week the teacher makes an arrangement whereby the farmer brings them back to the camp on Saturday night and comes for them the following night.

The people in the community in which the camp is located have established a nonsectarian church in an old cheese factory which has been purchased for $200. Occasionally a minister from a near-by town comes and speaks.

The camp has a professional cook, who was obtained from a college fraternity, and the boys pay pro rata. The first expense was about $2.50

a week for each boy, but prosperity has provided means for the boys to spend more.

All vegetables which the boys raised and which they did not use on the table were canned by the cook and Mrs. Rexford, and they will be used in the early part of next year, before the fresh vegetables are available.

Local store men have coöperated in giving the lowest prices, feeling that otherwise the trade of the camp would go to the city, and therefore choosing the opportunity of large business with aggregate large receipts on small profit.

Breakfast consists of fruit, cereal or eggs, and milk, cocoa, or postum, and sometimes corn bread or griddle cakes. The boys carry a cold lunch with them, consisting of a pail of cold cocoa; four good thick sandwiches of peanut butter, meat, or jam; a piece of frosted cake; and a banana. Sometimes they take a pot of jam, which is disposed of by the group. For dinner they have a roast or steak; potatoes and other ordinary vegetables (beans, peas, lettuce, carrots); shortcake or pie or pudding; cocoa, postum, or milk.

The boys take care of their own beds, wash the dishes, and keep the place clean.

They have a study hour every evening from eight until nine, and the same is true of the boys placed out with farmers. One boy, going to Princeton in the fall, kept up his studies and took the Regents' examinations at the country school, passing them with as good a mark as he would have obtained at his home school.

After drill on Sunday morning the boys at camp have a baseball game. They have had entertainments for the benefit of the Red Cross. In the group at camp are the gold-medal orator of the school, two excellent pianists, four mandolin players, and a whistler. All the boys are good singers.

Rexford's application blank asked for the weight, age, previous experience in farming, church preference, and habits as to smoking.

The teacher had the coöperation of the farm bureau. The farmers wrote to the bureau for help; Mr. Rexford and the farm-bureau manager went to each farmer, looked over the situation, and if everything was satisfactory, furnished the workers. Mr. Rexford will not leave boys on any farm without proper supervision. He visits the boys once every week, neither the farmer nor the boy knowing when he is coming.

At first no wage scale was set, the arrangement being that the farmer should pay what the boy was worth. If he was worth nothing, then it was all right, and the boy ought to be the first one to know it. However, most of the boys started at 20 cents an hour; soon this was raised to 25 cents, and now the pay is 30 cents.

Most of the farmers in the vicinity had never done any spraying. They now apply to Mr. Rexford when they want such work done and he sends out two boys and horses and his own spraying outfit. The work is done at a cost to the farmer of about 70 cents per acre for spraying potatoes, in addition to the material; that is, 25 cents per acre for each boy's work and 20 cents expense on the spraying outfit, for nozzles etc.

There was no illness among the boys during the summer, not even colds. Sometimes the boys got wet through, but came home, took a dip in a hole in the creek, and followed it by a good rub.

Meanwhile quite a number of New York City men teachers under the leadership of two camp supervisors, H. W. Millspaugh and H. J. McCreary, and acting under the authority of the Board of Education, started out "to sell something they did not have to somebody who did not want it." But these men had the courage of their convictions and the results of their work (over twenty camps in two counties) give ample evidence of the success of their venture.

Imagine the surprise of the fruit growers of the counties named when they received the following circular letter:

It is proposed to bring a large number of boys from the high schools of New York City to pick fruit in the fruit belt of Orange and Ulster counties. In carrying out this plan it will be necessary to have the full coöperation of fruit growers, school authorities, parents, health authorities, and others. The part of the fruit grower will be roughly as follows:

He will provide housing facilities, stove, fuel, refrigeration, either by ice box, cellar, or spring, convenient water supply, toilet facilities satisfactory to the board of health, straw for mattresses, cooking utensils, working conditions that will enable the average boy to earn a respectable wage, and a sympathetic attitude toward the comfort and health of the boys.

Each boy will provide his carfare to and from the fruit section, provide his own knife, fork, cup, plate, spoon, wash basin, tick for mattress, pillow, blankets, etc., and pay for his food and cooking. Boys will mess in groups of 12 to 25 or even more. Each group will have a capable boy cook and in camps of over 20, two boys. The first boy will receive $4 a week besides his meals, the second boy $2.50 a week and may earn some more by picking fruit. A teacher supervisor will supervise one large or two or three small camps and advise as to preparation of food, buy supplies, and act as camp director.

Regarding cooking outfit to be supplied by the fruit grower, it may be said that all except stove and ice box can

be purchased new for about $10. It is desirable that these
be ordered by the camp director, who will judge the size and
kind and take advantage of wholesale rates. An oil stove
and oven is recommended unless a suitable stove is on hand.
Inexperienced boy cooks cannot be expected to satisfy a
score or more of hungry boys with equipment discarded by
the skilled housewife.

It is further understood that these boys will not work on
Sunday nor will they be located on farms where farm help
is not treated with consideration.

An illustration of a "concentration and training
camp" is that established by the state of Maine.
This state, in coöperation with the state Young
Men's Christian Association, developed a state
camp for the purpose of enlisting and training
boys and young men to supply the extra demand
for farm labor made necessary through the in-
creased-acreage propaganda. The boys were organized under the title of "The Junior Volunteers
of Maine." They were virtually farm soldiers of
the state, and were sworn to obey all rules of the
camp before and after leaving it for the farms on
which they were placed.

The boys are sent out in squads to work in
different sections of the state, as opportunity may
offer, under the direction of competent adult leaders.
These leaders have full charge of the boys until
they return to the mobilization camp.

When a boy comes to the camp he is examined for his moral and physical qualifications, and then is assigned to a company and to a tent. The adjutant general provides necessary tents, uniforms, and camp utensils. The boy is instructed with others in the squad how to pitch a tent and pack camp utensils, and he is also given lessons in sanitation and the elements of military drill. He has a lecture every day given by a professor of the state agricultural college. He also works on the Y. M. C. A. farm, which is being used for this purpose, and is taught the use of machinery, and how to manage and care for horses, sharpen tools, and milk cows.

It is not claimed that a week of this sort of training makes the boy a finished farmer, but it does go a long way in that preliminary education so essential to farm-mindedness. By the time the boy gets to the farmer he is in excellent shape to understand the orders of his employer. In the words of the director of the camp, "He is ready to begin actual service as a trained novice."

Before the boy is admitted to the camp a searching examination is made into his character and antecedents, and some responsible person must answer certain confidential questions relative to the boy's physical, mental, and social habits.

After the boy is admitted to the camp he takes an oath in which he states that he will serve as a junior volunteer for farm service in Maine until the last day of October, unless sooner released by the governor of the state of Maine.

A charge is made on the farmer of $1 a day for each of the six working days, and it is expected that if the boys show themselves worthy of more, the farmer will recognize this and make a satisfactory adjustment with the leader. In addition to the minimum charge of $1 a day the farmer is required to furnish board. As a rule, however, the boys sleep in near-by tents with their leaders. The farmer is not required to pay transportation or other charges.

The farmer's agreement is with the state and not with the boy, as the scheme works on the basis that the young men have been engaged by the state for farm service and as employees of the state receive their pay through the regular state channels.

On the first of July more than 450 boys had been trained and sent out to various points in the state.

The following letter from the director-general of the camp gives in a word his experience with these boys:

We feel that this movement can be justified from any one of a half-dozen standpoints. We are taking city boys and in a few weeks giving them a few carefully selected fundamental principles relating to practical farm activities, which has enabled them to go out to the farms under our leaders and give satisfaction. We have not had a single complete failure yet. Only 3 boys out of 600 employed for the season have been changed because they could not fill the requirements. The way these city boys have taken hold of farm work has been wonderfully gratifying. In connection with this training, we are conducting our camp along lines similar to camps of National Guardsmen. The whole organization is nearly identical with the regular army camps. While the training is not so extensive, the boys are given the fundamentals in correct form. The spirit and general training at the camp will be of great value if any of these boys are ever called into the service.

Another important possibility, and from my experience with city boys, a probability, is that some of these boys will become sufficiently interested in agriculture to choose it as a vocation, while others will choose it later in life as an avocation, because of this experience.

Another mobilization camp of the "labor-distribution" type, with some training features, was that of the Long Island Food Reserve Battalion. This organization was initiated by the Nassau County Y.M.C.A. and supported financially and morally by the Long Island Railroad, the state agricultural school at Farmingdale, and by local residents. A detailed description is unnecessary. There were 6 camps under this organization scattered over the island, in each camp 48 boys under a supervisor, a military instructor, and squad leaders (1 squad leader to approximately every 7 boys). The last camp was developed at the state school of agriculture with a group of 96 boys working in two shifts, one beginning at 6 A.M. and stopping at 12 noon; the other beginning at 12 noon and stopping at 6 P.M. A regular course of agricultural instruction was carried on at all the camps. Lectures have been given in entomology, farm chemistry, and marketing. During the first month of the first camp it was difficult to place the boys. The idea was not well received by the farmers, who claimed that the presence of boys would "demoralize" their regular help, and that the boys would not recognize the different vegetables and would hoe out corn as quickly as they would pigweed. (One boy in a New York State camp did carefully hoe out and pull up every corn plant for a half-day, leaving weeds.)

During the height of the season these same farmers were driving to the camps and offering from $2 to $2.50 a day for the same boys that they had laughed at hiring for $1.25 a day at the beginning of the installation of the camps.

The "flying-squadron" idea is unique. An auto truck, with a trailer for tentage and supplies, is always ready to respond with its load of boys to an emergency call to save some particular crop. The group composing this squadron is made up of "hand-picked" boys who are qualifying for squad-leader positions.

An example of a camp which was conducted in such a manner that the boys lost the minimum of school work is that of the Bushwick (Brooklyn, New York), High School "Camp Squire" near Hicksville, Long Island. The organization of this camp is interesting, not so much because it was established with the purpose of making it self-supporting, but rather because it provided definite opportunities for continuing with school studies. The initial amount of about $175 was subscribed by teachers, and the tent and mess house, intended formerly for harvesters, was lent by the farmer on whose grounds the camp was placed. The leader of this camp, a teacher in the same school from which the boys were recruited, planned, after the schools opened in September, a day of work and study, coaching the boys in their school subjects, so that with at least three hours of study per day the boys were enabled to keep up with their classes while at work harvesting until the middle of October. In this, as in other successful camps, the boys formed a unit organization before going to camp, and had the advantage of a sympathetic instructor of academic and agricultural experience to enforce voluntary school discipline. The boys were paid 20 to 25 cents an hour, working for neighboring farmers from 7 A.M. to 3 P.M. The rest of the day was divided into silent study, consultation, and recreation hours. It is expected that this camp, which will doubtless be permanent, will become self-supporting in its second or third year and the initial outlay will be returned.

The farm-camp idea is here to stay. Of that we are sure. The purely recreational camp is a thing of the past. The days of the purely work camp of ten to twelve hours a day ought to be over. Work, play, and study in the future will be brought together in the summer time as effectively as during the so-called "regular" season. Next year, and in the years after, we shall organize this work around some educational ideal and not merely around a necessity for food-production. The two are by no means incompatible.

This year we have learned "how not to do it," as one camp leader put it. In some instances the boys went home with less money than they had at the start. In brief they paid the farmer for the privilege of picking berries. Particularly in berry picking there was much piece work, and such may carry with it nearly all the evils that it does in the factory. Mr. Keller, a thoughtful leader of a New York camp, says in this connection: "Judging the fair wage from the earnings of the expert is manifestly unfair. It means that the average boy must be speeded up beyond his point of endurance, or that he must receive less than a living wage. The possibilities of speeding up are limited, and so the alternative is longer hours."

Furthermore it is necessary for the government, state or national, to take a hand in the distribution and the sale of farm products. It made me sick at heart, on a trip of inspection to 25 camps, to see hundreds of boys at work picking berries under the hot sun in a service supposedly patriotic, and then to see the same berries, which had been sold by the growers at a price not much above that of other years, resold to the consumer at double the price of other years, — and always with the remark: "You know labor is scarce this year, and the farmers cannot get help." The result of it all has been that the consumer, for whom the work was done, has been disregarded.

From the point of view of social reconstruction, education, food production, and conservation only the surface has been scratched. The state must take the initiative, assuring the consumer a moderate price for the product, and the farmer, the dealer, and the boy a fair return for their service.

The boy is not merely a labor unit in the conservation of food. He is the essential feature of an educational program. The experience of the past summer proves that with centralization, organization, and an educational vision as fundamental subdivisions of a far-sighted state policy the placing of boy labor on farms could become a valuable and permanent by-product of the war.

CHAPTER XI

THE ORGANIZATION OF A CADET CAMP

In organizing camps for supplying cadet labor it is well to keep in mind that they are to be established on the basis of a business proposition; that they are not primarily play camps or recreational camps; that they are not to be located on a river or lake because there happens to be a good place for boys to swim, if there are not paying jobs near that river or lake on which the boys may work; that they are not to be established at random without reference to the continuity of work during the season, or without any real knowledge of the local demand for labor.

Out of considerable experience during the past year it has been discovered that there are three great elements: first, the boy; second, the farmer; and third, the job. In addition there are the elements of leadership, of housing, and of cooking. Of course there must also be considered the elements of recreation, religious observances, and the general social life of the camp.

With reference to the boy it would seem that he ought to be one of a group which belongs to a public-school system, or to an institution, or to some society or organization which is ready to coöperate in placing him in a farm camp. We are hardly prepared as yet to take individual boys, unassociated with any organization, and bring them together in a camp where the lack of unity will give the leader little hold. A number of boys from New York City were picked up at random and sent out to a distant place up-state under the direction of a leader who had never seen them before. The boys had not met one another until they were put on a train in New York. Not coming from any single school or organization, they felt no particular responsibility to anyone. All they knew about the proposition was that they were to go to a certain place, where they would be met by someone who was to conduct them to a camp. They were undisciplined and later proved to be unmanageable. At the very start the plan lacked that coördinating influence which would have existed if the leader had been a teacher in a school from which these boys had come as one group, or if a Y.M.C.A. boys' secretary had organized a group from his association. Of course, some day a way may be found to bring together a group of boys independent of previous association and place them in a new environment in about the same way that adult labor is gathered up in the streets of New York and shipped by employment agencies to some distant point. But boys are not men. The responsibility of sending a more or less irresponsible youth to a distant point by the same methods that are used by employment agencies in sending men is too great for any state or community to undertake.

It is generally understood that the best boys for farm work are those who are over 16 years of age. This is true, of course, of boys who engage in general farm work, such as plowing, milking, horse cultivating, haying, and harvesting grains and potatoes. Many such boys were placed in the dairying and general-farming regions of New York State. These boys, in most cases, lived with the individual farmer and were paid by the month. But it has been found from experience that the 14-year-old boy is often better adapted to certain types of farm work than is the older boy. For example, the young boy, with his adolescent enthusiasm, his nimbler fingers, and his general physical alertness, is more desirable for picking small fruits, such as strawberries, currants, raspberries, blackberries, gooseberries, and cherries. *The 14-year-old boy must, however, work on a different basis from the one who is over 16.*

It is necessary for the boys to pass a physical examination, because no state authorities care to assume the responsibility of taking the physically unfit. It is taken for granted that the boy is to fit into the organization of the camp as a business proposition and that he is to stick to his work, pay his share of the cost of the food and its preparation, respond to leadership, and in every way do his part toward promoting the general efficiency of the camp.

The enlistment blank used by the New York State Military Training Commission is shown on page 276.

The farmer is as important an element as the boy; yes, even more important, for the boy gradually loses his individuality in the camp conscience. The individual farmer remains an individual. He has his notions of what boys can do; he compares the work of the inexperienced boy with the adult foreign labor which he has previously employed. The latter has, until very recently, been available. Women with their children came to his farm and picked the small fruits without much regard to the length of the day's work or to living conditions, and, of course, without any reference to the social life of the community. This labor went out as it came in. If it did not like the job because the pay was insufficient, it demanded higher wages and got them or left the job and moved on to the next one.

NEW YORK STATE MILITARY TRAINING COMMISSION
BUREAU OF VOCATIONAL TRAINING
ENLISTMENT AS FARM CADET

Name_____

Residence_____ Street

Age_____yr. Height_____ft.____in. Weight_____lb.

Place of enlistment_____
(Name of institution, club, or association)

I desire to enlist for farm work and will report for service:	Kind of work desired; as picking fruit, vegetable gardening, general farming, etc.
From mo.___day___to mo.___day___ From mo.___day___to mo.___day___	

Can you drive a team?_____ Can you milk?_____

Can you drive an automobile?_____

State briefly any other farm experience you have had.

I have examined the applicant and do assert that he is physically fit to do farm work.

_____
(Physician's signature)

I permit_____ to enlist for farm work as

stated above _____
(Parent or guardian)

It did not mind shacks which lodged vermin. It was not particular about sanitary conveniences; it was not particular about anything except wages. In shifting from adult foreign labor to boy labor,

the farmer was obliged to readjust his mental attitude. Not only that, but he often had to readjust
the physical, economic, and social conditions on
his farm.

In April, at the time the New York agricultural
census was taken, the farmer said that he needed
labor. He even said he would take boy labor, but
when it came actually to engaging such labor, he
was inclined to ridicule the idea. Untrained city
boys were not in great demand in May, but when
the foreign labor did not appear on the scene and
strawberries were ripening on the vines, the farmer
suddenly discovered that he could use the untrained
city boy. But he had expected the boys not only
to work as many hours but also to pick as carefully and as much as adults. He expected the boys
to work at the same price as had foreigners for
years past, regardless of the advance in price of
food and the standards of living. Of course he was
disappointed, and this is where the leader of the
camp, through his authority, represents the interests of the boys and the newer conditions of farm
labor which have come out of the employment
of boys.

An instance of what happened in Highland,
New York, will illustrate the power of leadership
on the part of a camp leader and the coöperative

instinct of a group of city boys who have considerable familiarity with the principles of strikes, lockouts, picket duty, and street-corner oratory. The boys were being paid one and one-half cents a quart for currant picking. In years past this had been the usual rate. They could, on the average, pick about 40 quarts a day, which brought them $3.60 a week, assuming that they worked for six days in the week and there was no rain or other interruptions. Meanwhile each boy's proportion of the board at camp amounted to about $3.50 a week. At this point a combination of training in school debating, listening to speeches of industrial disturbers, and a knowledge of trade-union methods came into play, for these boys gathered together and determined to demand two cents a quart. They held a meeting and voted to strike for two cents. They marched around the berry-storage houses, each wearing an empty berry basket as a cap, on which was marked "two cents" and which was decorated more or less artistically with bunches of currants. A meeting of all farmers of the district was called by the general camp supervisor of the district. The boys had presented their arguments to the individual camp leaders, and in turn the supervisor presented them to the farmers. The farmers, in turn, presented their difficulties. They said they could not afford to pay more; talked about middlemen, commission-men, express rates, greater cost of baskets and crates, mortgage on the farm, and everything, in fact, except the federal income tax. But the boys won out, and the meeting resulted in a new price never before paid for picking currants. And the boys who, up to then, had been able to pick only 40 quarts a day, were able to gather many more after the advance in rate, picking 60 quarts a day instead of 40 quarts. There are people who can read into this short story an economic principle.

It is absolutely necessary to have a clear under-standing between the boy-camp group, through its leader or the organization sending the camp, and the individual farmer or the group of farmers employing the boys, as to fundamental points of remuneration, type of work expected, length and permanency of service.

The boy-camp-group problem is wholly different from the problem of the individual boy who works for an individual farmer and has no established relations with any camp. The latter is a contract relationship between the boy and the farmer. The farmer usually hires the boy by the month for general farm work, and the duties incident to such a job are familiar to everyone. The hours may be long or short, the work hard or easy, the food good or bad, the boy's room clean or unsanitary; but there is nothing unusual in this problem.

The one which is discussed here is that of the labor camp, where a group of boys are projected into a strange community to work at a job unfamiliar to the majority of them,— working for a farmer or a group of farmers who have never before employed such a type of labor. Any single employer of farm labor who is in a position to employ a group of boys may be assumed either to be conducting a large farm on which there is a great diversity of crops extending over a wide range of time of harvesting, or to be a specializing farmer working in an intensive way on a comparatively small area with special crops which are harvested in short periods of time. Perhaps it may be better to think of three types of jobs, or rather, three types of employers who have jobs to be filled by groups of boys.

First, there is the individual farmer who is a specialist. Such employers grow berries and other small fruits. Here the boys get very little farm experience. They do obtain an idea of country life, and they have excellent camp experience, but in order to learn much about the fruit and berry business they ought to be on the farm during the time of spraying, pruning, and fertilizing. In reality these boys are but factory hands under farm conditions. Of course this type of work is extremely well adapted to the inexperienced boy.

Second, there is the type of employer represented by the vegetable grower. In this case it is readily seen that crops are put into the ground as early as April, and seeding may continue until the fifteenth of August, and with weeding, thinning, and cultivating, the work may continue practically throughout the season. The harvesting of certain crops may start late in June and continue until the ground freezes. In this work the boys obtain the very best sort of farm experience outside of that obtained from general farm work. The work which they do is diversified, and they learn about many farm operations.

Third, another type of employer is the business organization made up of farmers; as, for example, the shippers' or growers' association, where a group of farmers unite under a more or less compact organization for the purpose of raising and moving crops. Another illustration — somewhat different for the reason that the organization is not made up of farmers, but rather is allied with farmers — is that of a canning company. In working for such a type of employer the boy may or may not gain considerable agricultural experience, depending entirely upon whether he is working on diversified crops for long periods of time or doing specialized harvesting. It is necessary to keep in mind these different types of work as represented by different types of employers.

It is clear that in some sections, under certain agricultural conditions already described, the job might be guaranteed a group of boys from the middle of April until the first of November, with almost steady work for six days in the week. The nature of crops and weather conditions determine continuity of work. A heavy rain means a good deal of cultivating and weeding immediately afterward in order to conserve the moisture. A light rain means that the boys can work for part of the day in the fields, while in the case of small-fruit farming even a slight rain prevents the picking of the fruit. Again, in vegetable farming a boy may work all day if the fields are not too hot, without any injury to his health or to the crops, because the vegetable plants cannot be injured by handling, no matter how hot it is.

In the case of the specialized farmer, there is little or no guarantee for work beyond a short and definite period; that is, the period is necessarily short, but whether or not it is definite depends a great deal upon the weather and prices of crops. It is obvious that an abundant crop might cause a low market price,— a price too low to pay for picking,— and employers who early in the season thought that they wanted a group of boys might decline to accept them at the last moment. They might even contract for the boy-labor camp and after the boys had picked for a few days desire to drop the whole enterprise because of a fall in the market price,— a fall which would not be evident until the crops commenced to come. Or, again, the employer might contract for a camp of boys to pick strawberries, for example, and complete arrangements might be made for bringing the boys to the locality, only to have the camp project abandoned because a week of rain had absolutely ruined the strawberry crops. Such an experience was met in New York State the past season. A hailstorm in Chautauqua County completely destroyed in a few minutes the prospects of a camp for the harvesting of tomatoes. Now, it is evident that it is a difficult matter always to guarantee a job.

The Bureau of Vocational Training of the Military Training Commission of New York State requested the zone representatives in the farm-placement bureaus to see to it that jobs were guaranteed to boys and that the time of service, place of service, and pay should be clearly stated. It furthermore recommended that the job should be guaranteed in writing by a single farmer, by a group of farmers, or by the corporation desiring these boys; that the employing party should state the kind of work, the pay, the number of boys needed, the duration of service, the living conditions, the provisions made for the food supply for the first week, and so on. It made it clear that there should be an assurance in writing of what the boys were to expect, and that someone should be delegated to see that the employer lived up to his agreement. Out of a theory not based upon any previous experience it was obviously easy to write up such a statement, but to expect it to be carried out without a hitch in all parts of the state and for all kinds of work and all types of employers, not taking into consideration climatic and market conditions, to say nothing about the prejudices and idiosyncrasies of employers and boys, was to count the chickens before they were hatched. About all that can be said at this stage of this movement is in illustration of the way the job guarantee was handled. In what follows it must be kept in mind that much of what has been said or what may be said about the proposition of guaranteeing the job is not at all difficult to carry out in the case of general farming and is only moderately difficult in the case of vegetable growing.

Every camp failure due to the lack of a workable contract justifies the original contention that guaranteeing the job is extremely important.

MEMORANDUM OF UNDERSTANDING IN REFERENCE TO THE SOUTH LIMA (NEW YORK) CAMP

Between the New York State Military Training Commission Farm-Cadet Bureau, West Central Zone (Nathaniel G. West, Field Inspector, Rochester, New York) and the Growers' and Shippers' Association of South Lima, New York.

The Farm-Cadet Bureau, West Central Zone, agrees :

1. To furnish 25 or more unskilled farm cadets, 16 to 19 years of age, for labor on muck and upland farms.

2. To furnish a camp leader, who shall have general charge of the camp of boys, who shall hire out the boys to near-by farmers, collect all wages, and purchase supplies.

3. That the camp leader shall keep an accurate account of all wages paid to farm cadets and percentage collected, such accounts to be open for inspection by committee designated by the Growers' and Shippers' Association.

4. To furnish a competent camp cook who shall prepare all meals for the farm cadets.

5. To pay each week, through the camp leader, to the Growers' and Shippers' Association a sum for overhead expenses, as explained below, — such sum to be procured by adding to all wages earned by the cadets a sum equal to five per cent of such wages.

The Growers' and Shippers' Association agrees:

1. To provide work, as continuously as possible, for each of the farm cadets in the above camp from June 11, 1917, to November 3, 1917.

2. To pay wages for each farm cadet at the rate of $2 per day's work, such day's work not to exceed ten hours.

3. To pay at the end of such week to the camp leader all wages earned by farm cadets during that week.

4. To pay in addition to the above wages a sum equal to 5 per cent of the wages, such sum to be turned over to treasurer of the Growers' and Shippers' Association for payment of overhead expenses of the camp.

5. To arrange for rental of suitable quarters for the cadets, furnish two ranges and fuel for same, furnish 27 or more cots, tables, benches, and chairs for the quarters, install a telephone, and arrange with local grocer for two weeks' credit for the camp leader for the purchase of supplies.

6. To pay for the items mentioned under 5, above, out of the 5 per cent received from the camp leader, as agreed above.

MASSACHUSETTS PLAN OF INDIVIDUAL AGREEMENT WITH FARMER

To the Committee on Food Production and Conservation

(Department of Mobilization of Schoolboys for Farm Service)

Dear Sirs:

I hereby apply for _____ boys to be employed by me as general farm labor according to the terms and regulations on the reverse side of this application.

I shall require these boys to begin work upon _____ _____ and probably require their services, if satisfactory, until _____

I agree to pay each boy $4 per week for the first two weeks, and $6 per week thereafter; such payment to be made on Saturday of each week. (Afterwards changed, see chapter on "Farm Cadets," p. 250.)

If the boy lives in a camp, I agree to pay $4 per week for his board, and if he lives with me, I will furnish his board; the above to be in addition to his wages.

I agree to employ the boy on rainy days as well as fair days, and on rainy days to use his service as far as possible under cover.

I agree, if the boy is unsatisfactory, to give him one week's notice or one week's pay, providing him with a statement in writing giving my reasons for his discharge.

Whenever in the opinion of the local supervisor, the conditions of living or of labor are not satisfactory, the boy may be withdrawn without prejudice to him.

The nature of the work for which the boy is required is

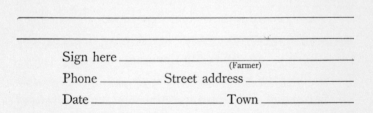

Sign here _____
                          (Farmer)

Phone _____ Street address _____

Date _____ Town _____

The right leadership in a camp is very essential. The camp, after all, is but the lengthened shadow of its leader. It is not difficult to write the qualifications essential to leadership in a boys' farm camp, but it is another matter to find any one person who will fill all the conditions that are peculiar to a labor camp. A hundred-point man capable of measuring up to the problems involved in camp leadership must have had experience in school or Association work. He would have knowledge of cooking utensils and personal equipment necessary to take to camp; capacity to arrange for transportation for the boys by the most direct, convenient, and economical route; ability to deal successfully with the problem of the first night in camp, — a night when boys cannot or will not sleep, when they are stirred up by the novelty of the situation. He would be able to recognize good, substantial, nourishing food, and to see that the boys had proper food in such an emergency as the camp cook's suddenly being taken ill or deserting his job. He would have had experience in adjusting working conditions, would know how many quarts of fruit, for example, the average boy can pick; would be able to help these boys get the most out of their work by showing them the most effective method of harvesting; would understand how to use first-aid equipment. He would have to see that the boys kept up correspondence with their homes. He might have to sit up all night with a boy who had eaten more fruit than was good for him.

The right leader will also have to think of reading

matter for the camp and of the problem of having the boys attend church services on Sunday when the membership of the camp has varied religious beliefs. He may have some orthodox Jews in camp when the country village has only a Methodist church. He must satisfy the boys who want to have a minstrel show, or the townspeople who offer to entertain the boys. He may even have to arbitrate in labor disputes. He may be the local placement bureau. He should be able to drive an automobile, in order that he may carry a flying squad five miles from camp for a day's work for a farmer who is in immediate need. He must be able to answer the questions asked on blanks sent out by the state departments of agriculture and education, by city boards of education, by state Y.M.C.A.'s, by child-labor bureaus, and by all other organizations more or less directly interested in the new aspects of old problems. If the boys have been excused from school, he must certify that their labor-camp work has been equivalent to the school work which they otherwise would have had. He must be the banker of the camp and help the boys conserve the money which they earn. He is accountable to the group for the expenses of the camp, in order that these may be divided pro rata. He must be able to buy supplies at the least cost.

It is with deliberate intention that this list has been made lengthy and of wide range, in order to show that no man exists who could meet adequately every condition imposed. He is bound to be " born short," as William Hawley Smith would state it, on some of these angles. If he is a social-minded man of the Boy Scout or Y.M.C.A. type, he will be long on entertainments, recreation, food require- ments, knowledge of personal equipment, group work, first aid, and sanitation. If he is of the school-teacher type, he will probably be strong on discipline, efficient in looking after details of school credits, camp expenses, records, moral conditions, letter writing, and keeping boys busy. If he is a technical man in agriculture, he may know nothing about baseball on Saturday afternoon or how to organize a minstrel show, but he will probably know how to do more than keep boys busy. He will keep them effectively busy; that is, he will arrange to have certain boys do the lines of work adapted to their skill and knowledge. He will dis- cover ways of utilizing the labor of the unskilled boy. He will be able to judge whether or not a boy is working to his full capacity, and he may be somewhat pitiless if the boy does not measure up to a farm-labor standard. In other words, such a man will be very largely interested in a working camp. He will be interested in meeting the conditions imposed by the farmers. He will know that the berries must be expressed by four o'clock and that the picking may have to stop promptly at two. He will know that a leaky crate of raspberries means a low price for possibly a whole carload. He will be less interested, perhaps, in the balanced ration and more interested in using the products of the community on the camp table. He will not be interested in the records required by school officials so much as in those expected of him by the farm-bureau agent. In short, his idea is to promote agriculture and not to promote the county Y.M.C.A. movement, the back-to-the-farm movement, or any other movement which may be allied with the farm-cadet service.

It is not possible to find any one man who is socially, pedagogically, and agriculturally minded. If he claims to be good in all three fields he probably is mediocre. The experience of the past year, however, shows some remarkably fine work done by leaders of boy camps. Some have been public-school teachers who have given their summer services for nothing or for a nominal fee. Some have been released from their duties as Y.M.C.A. secretaries in order that the association might make a contribution to the farm-cadet movement. Some have been physical directors in public schools. Some have been scout masters among the Boy Scouts. Others have been agricultural teachers who saw that this work was, after all, in the line of their usual duties.

The following illustrates one of the hundred things which a camp leader must know about:

INSTRUCTIONS TO FARM CADETS ENLISTED FOR CAMP-SQUAD SERVICE IN NEW YORK STATE

WHAT TO TAKE

NECESSARY ARTICLES

Bed sack 75 × 30 inches (to be stuffed with straw at camp) or cot mattress; enamel-ware plate, cup, saucer, sauce dish, also knife, fork, and spoon; dinner pail or box, two heavy blankets, small pillow, working clothes, sweater, gymnasium shirt, raincoat or old overcoat, heavy shoes, toothbrush, tooth powder, small mirror, towels, extra socks, rubbers or rubber boots, extra underwear, hairbrush, comb, soap, handkerchiefs, pajamas, a good disposition, and a spirit of loyalty to the camp and its aims.

DESIRABLE ARTICLES

Musical instruments, camera, baseball, glove, bat, needles, thread, safety pins, notebook, pencils, writing paper, envelopes, good books, magazines.

The methods of housing the boys differ widely. Ordinarily one thinks of tents as being the most feasible, but the scarcity and high cost of such equipment during the past year prevented the boys from living under canvas. Generally speaking, it would be better to think in terms of something more permanent than tents, as these do not last more than three years, and if the camp idea of harvesting crops by the use of boys is to continue, — and many believe it will, — it is advisable to plan for a permanent and inexpensive type of building. A rough board shack with a good roof is highly desirable in the early spring days and in the late fall.

Many of the cadets in New York State camps were quartered in berry houses (which are really packing and storage houses located in the berry fields), in vacant houses, in schoolhouses, in grange halls, and in buildings located on the fair grounds. Most of these berry houses were two stories high, the first floor being used for the commissary department and the second floor for dormitories. In such cases the berries were packed in temporary shacks adjoining the berry houses. In other cases the boys have used the first floor for a sitting room and built a rough shack back of the berry or storage house for kitchen and dining room.

One of the most significant camping places was that of a two-room schoolhouse, where cots for fifty boys were put into the rooms, and the basement was used as a kitchen. The boys built a table outside and put up a canopy over it for a dining room.

They next dammed up a brook which ran back of the schoolhouse and made what they termed a "bathtub," which was capable of holding about six boys at a time. They also put into fine condition the rather disreputable schoolhouse latrines. These boys made the schoolhouse ring at night with their popular school songs; the old piano did its best to bring together the heritages of the East Side and of the Highlands of the Hudson.

There are several ways of making provision for camp equipment. One is to develop, under state, county, or local auspices, a series of permanent camp quarters located in small-fruit, large-fruit, and muck-land districts. This equipment need not be expensive. It will be located very near the source of labor demand and can always be used, whether boy or adult labor is employed. Fruit and produce growers and kindred establishments have in the past provided, more or less, for such an equipment.

Another plan is to use schoolhouses, grange halls, vacant farm buildings, and agricultural-fair equipment. It is unfortunate that so much property ordinarily used for public purposes lies idle for long periods of time. Some may say that the city boy will not leave country property in good shape, but experience so far has shown that the city boys have left things better than they found them.

Still another type already spoken of is tentage, and perhaps the best way to provide such an equipment is to have the state furnish it through the adjutant general's office.

The sanitary aspects of any type of camp are highly important. In Massachusetts the committee of public safety, which established boy camps, required that the sanitary conditions of these camps should be inspected by the board of health, and the committee furnished full directions and a blue print for the building of a sanitary latrine.

Some of the camps burn their garbage in home-made incineration plants.

Ordinary garden hose with a watering-pot sprinkler attachment, or an elevated barrel with a sprayer attached, and filled by the use of a pail and ladder, were shower-bath devices worked out by the boys in various camps.

All the camps devised some method of keeping food cool, ranging from those that had a real city ice chest down to those that cleaned out a spring and set in it a bottomless, covered box.

The job of feeding boys in camp is not a sinecure. Every scheme has been tried, from engaging at a salary of one hundred dollars a month a Pullman dining-car chef down to, or shall it be said up to, a boy cook. The cook problem in a labor camp is as difficult to handle as is the so-called "servant" problem of the city. The average cook knows more about cooking than he does about dietetics. He is very likely to lack adaptability. He is usually untrained for camp cooking and is not particularly open to suggestions. Experience seems to show that the best cook is the one who has done work in a Y.M.C.A. camp or in a Boy Scout camp. Of course, this year there was a great scarcity of the latter class to be found, as they were needed in their own organizations, and therefore many camps were obliged to employ a local woman of the matronly type to cook for the boys; sometimes an experienced camp leader has developed some good cooks among the boys in camp. Perhaps the best results, however, were obtained from boys who before the opening of camps were given from two to four weeks of camp-cooking instruction in the school system from which they came. These boys were ready to use the products of the localities, such as peas, beans, tomatoes, radishes, lettuce, and corn, while the professional cook often seemed more familiar with the use of the can opener.

The quantity and variety of food was practically in the hands of the boys themselves, assuming that the cook was a good one. If the allowance of fruit for breakfast, for example, consisted of four prunes or one banana or half an orange, and the group as a whole desired a larger portion, it was perfectly possible for them to secure it by so voting, for it must be remembered that the food expense of the camps was divided pro rata among the boys. Under these conditions, however, it was found that the boys were very economical and frowned upon the few malcontents who wanted to gorge themselves.

The cafeteria style of serving prevailed generally.

Providing amusements in recreation camps is always a problem, but farm cadets require little in the way of entertainment after eight or ten hours of field service. Camp-fire talks on agriculture, corn roasts, toasting marshmallows, giving musical entertainments and minstrel shows, holding mock trials, playing baseball on Saturday afternoons or Sundays, constitute the chief forms of recreation. In every instance the lads have been well received in the local communities. They were popular features at church entertainments, Red Cross benefits, and country sociables. Often the boys, especially in the berry-picking regions, went swimming about 4 P.M., after the crates had been sent by the afternoon express.

In every instance the village church and the county Y.M.C.A. took an active interest in the farm cadets. Many of the boys played musical instruments, and their confidence in themselves was contributory to many supplementary boy choirs. The country pastors evidently made it a point to do what they could for the pleasure of all the boys, and without exception there seemed to be no religious distinctions. In some camps the Catholic priest expressed his fatherly feeling for the lads. In others the Jewish and Catholic boys attended the union village church. In brief, the boys entered into the spirit of the rural life, and both the country folk and the youth of the city were the better for it.

A study of the different camps in operation in various parts of the country seems to indicate that they might be grouped under six heads as follows.

I. *Concentration, or training, camps.* These are usually located in agriculturally strategic sections of the state, where boys may receive preliminary training in camp life and in farm work under disciplinary and instructional conditions. Of course such a camp can do nothing more than give the boys a training in the elements of farm activities (such as harnessing a horse, running a hand cultivator, using a hoe, driving a team) and serve as a trying-out period for weeding out boys who are unsatisfactory. These camps cannot be considered places which will give a preliminary agricultural education, for that is very different from giving a preliminary idea of farm operations. After these boys have received a course of such training, they are sent out under leadership to work in a section of the state where a group may work for one farmer and live at the camp meanwhile or may work for individual farmers and live with the employer. Obviously it is taken for granted that such a camp is located in a good agricultural section and that its surroundings have something more than fine swimming holes or beautiful scenery. These boys must be trained in an environment and under conditions similar to the farm life in which they are to participate later. It would seem that the agricultural colleges of the country and the secondary schools of agriculture would, generally speaking, offer splendid locations for establishing training camps. Here would be found, or ought to be found, good land. This is not always true, because occasionally an agricultural college has been located irrespective of good land. The technical and dormitory facilities, however, would be available for the boys in training.

II. *Farm-working, or labor-distributing, camps.* These are concentration camps in a certain sense, but they are located directly in the farm district where the boys, after receiving their preliminary training, are to find work in the community adjoining the camp. Several camps of this order have started out with the idea of giving a preliminary training in agriculture in the camp itself, and have borrowed or bought farming implements and teams and leased land in order to give the training. But in the majority of cases this idea was abandoned, for it was found that these boys could receive all their preliminary training with the farmers, provided the leader of the camp could establish helpful relations between the boy and the employing farmer and could, out of his wisdom and experience, protect the boy in the early stages of the work and guide him in all its stages. In other words, in this type of camp a city man, acting as leader, comes into a community with a group of boys who live at the camp but receive their training with the near-by farmers. A labor-supply camp, composed of able-bodied boys, is a type which adequately meets the need at small expense.

III. *Military farm-training camp.* This is a type of camp where city boys, under the direction of a school or some organization, go into a farming community and open up new land which otherwise would not have been put under cultivation. These boys stay at the camp during the season. They do not work for the farmers near by, or, at least, not ordinarily, — the intention being to establish a self-supporting and self-maintaining camp for the use of the boys who attend. The land is tilled, the seed planted, and the harvest gathered for the benefit of the boys. Any profits are given to the boys or to the school, and any expenses for conducting the camp, or overhead charges, usually come out of the organization or school represented. It is questionable whether, generally speaking, this type of camp is on a sound economic and agricultural basis. If such a camp could be carried on for a number of years with a strong school or other organization behind it, and plenty of capital, it is very likely that it would succeed. It takes capital to establish good soil conditions and purchase tools, farm machinery, and stock, and to put up buildings. It is a highly desirable type of camp to consider in terms of many years or where a school wishes to give its boys a military and farm experience. But in the food emergency through which the country is now passing, it is doubtful if this type of camp should ever have been started. It is, however, an excellent type to establish as a permanent adjunct to a city school system.

IV. *Coöperative camp where the boys share in proceeds.* This type of camp is practically like III, and if the farm land is new and the camp leader is untrained in agricultural operations and the boys are unskilled, it is about as likely to be doomed to failure as is the other.

V. *The village- or country-school type of camp.* This is a camp where the schoolboys, under the leadership of a teacher, go to the outskirts of the village and develop a garden. If the land is good and the teacher knows agriculture and the boys attend to business, they will most certainly receive an excellent practical training useful to them in life. They will have learned how to work in the soil, how to work together for a common purpose, how to stick to a job until it is finished, how to look ahead from the time seed is purchased until the crop is placed in the hands of the customer. All these things are good and they are useful to any boy, but, of course, from the standpoint of increasing the food supply in any large way through the growing of wheat, feed corn, oats, rye, buckwheat, potatoes, and large fruits there is little to be said. The work is to be commended on the basis of its value to the individual boy.

VI. *Short-term camp, sometimes called "flying squadron."* This type of camp is advisable only in an intensive-farming region where quick service for the harvesting period is needed. The squad itself will serve to keep a balance between the demand for labor and the supply. It is easy to picture a fruit region around and through which are a number of camps. Each one ought to be working to the limit, but, of course, as a matter of fact in one section there would be a greater demand for boys than could be met by the local camp. It is at this time that the flying squadron comes in, when, in response to the SOS call, a group of temporarily idle boys from one camp may be sent to another camp which is short of help.

CHAPTER XII

A SUMMARIZED PROGRAM OF ACTION

Out of this war we are going to have a new spirit and method in education. England has already begun to evaluate its present system. It has issued a report on the assistance which education, if properly directed, can give to industry and commerce after the war. The results of a recent investigation afford — so the report states — a convincing proof of the necessity of improving and extending the provisions hitherto made for instruction and training in scientific studies as a necessary foundation for fruitful research.

The report goes on to say that, in a sense unknown to former generations, England has become a part of Europe; and in the interest not merely of commerce but of the intelligent conduct of national affairs an adequate knowledge of the languages — and, through the languages, of the literatures, histories, and civilizations of European countries — should be in the possession of a far larger proportion of its population than in the past. It states that particular subjects of instruction in the high

Military engineering will become a popular and necessary part of the curricula of our colleges and technical institutes. A class in suspension-bridge work at Wentworth Institute, Boston, Massachusetts

Military preparedness of college boys and schoolboys includes other activities than merely drilling. Trench drainage, one of a score of war emergency courses, at Wentworth Institute, Boston, Massachusetts

Returned convalescent soldiers, who would be idle but for the opportunity offered to brush up their education. Ogden Military Convalescent Hospital

A corner of the printing and photo-engraving shop at Manitoba Military Convalescent Hospital, Winnipeg. These men have been assigned to courses of reëducation because of inability to return to their former occupations

schools and institutes cannot be divorced from the consideration of their organization and of their curricula as a whole, if a proper balance of studies is to be secured and if higher education is to be truly liberal and humane in its spirit and influence. It insists that access to the schools must be rendered easier for native ability wherever it is found, and affirms again and again that the needs of the nation cannot be satisfied merely by changes affecting higher education or by a provision of educational facilities confined to scholars of special gifts and abilities. It closes by saying that the future will make new and increased demands, especially in a democratic community, on the health, character, and intelligence of every citizen; and these demands can only be met by comprehensive and far-reaching improvements and developments of elementary education.

The individual-industrial-efficiency idea which we obtained from Germany will have to be interpreted in America not for military purposes, but in terms of personal and vocational service for the nation. Just as the academic militarism of the Old World has been found wanting and has been gradually transformed into the mobilization of all forces behind the lines on an entirely new basis and conception of what may be done by a people in time of war, so we in this country shall learn that we may in times of peace, through efficient and effective living, prepare for defense. In this preparation we may learn that improved elementary education, that vocational training, that bringing into the schools the Boy Scout spirit, that teaching of sanitation and personal hygiene, that organizing our courses on a unit and project basis, that developing systems of student service in school life, that extending school facilities to adults, and a hundred other things which have been thought of as fads and pedagogical idiosyncrasies will, to quote the New York State law relative to military equivalents, "specifically prepare for service useful to the state in the maintenance of defense, in the promotion of public safety, in the conservation and development of the state's resources, or in the construction and maintenance of public improvements." Truly, a program for peace as well as for war.

The school board and its executive officer, the superintendent, should do everything to save the school buildings for school purposes. They are literally factories turning out, it is hoped, handmade products; and in time of war their service should be increased rather than diminished. To use them as hospitals will be a mistake, — better by far confiscate department stores. Bring the war into the schools in the spirit already interpreted in preceding chapters, but do not take the schools into the war.

Do not eliminate studies indiscriminately. Evaluate if you will, — and this is always well, — but wholesale cutting out is to be avoided. It may be that the cost and value of instruction in freehand drawing will have to be compared with the permanent value of the study of Latin. It may be that instead of adding to the vocational department a machine-shop equipment, which is always expensive, it will be discovered that a coöperative course can be developed, employing the equipment of a neighboring factory, and that all the school need furnish is a teacher for blackboard work in mathematics, drawing, and science. It is likely that a longer school day will be advisable and also a longer school year. It is quite probable that the introduction of the methods of the Boy Scout movement into the public schools will be found superior to some of the present teaching of nature study, recreational work, civics, and conduct.

Provision must be made for filling the places of the male teachers who will be drafted. Many of these will be instructors in science and mathematics. It ought to be possible to secure the services of retired civil or mechanical engineers for teaching these subjects. It is feasible to draft into service married women who have once taught. It is to be hoped that the government will eventually recognize that educational enterprise as well as industrial enterprise ought to furnish grounds for exemption. As war comes closer to us provision must be made for keeping the schools open twelve months in the year, and from eight in the morning until ten at night for six days in the week. Every child up to the age of 14 must be kept in school. It is the best place for him, provided, of course, the school rises to its full height, — and it is taken for granted that it will. The physical condition of the younger children especially should be watched very carefully. The teacher should discover the conditions at home. It may be that some pupils have had no breakfast and are not likely to have a suitable lunch or even a supper. Some will have to be fed in the schools, and here is an opportunity for the older girls in domestic-science classes. Some will report certain home conditions that will require that the school make a report to the local Red Cross chapter or some other relief agency. Again there is opportunity for the older girls to serve through their knowledge of home nursing, infant feeding, and first aid.

If the war strikes us hard, we may have to think of part-time work for children above 14, but we must never let the children get away from us as they have in England. We must control the exodus. We must not abrogate the existing compulsory-attendance laws and the existing labor laws. We must not interpret these laws with laxity and shut our eyes while the children go by us on their way to work. We may do well to amend these laws if in so doing we can incorporate useful labor into the educative process. In other words, we must be constructive in any part-time measures which are adopted. The educative value of profitable labor need not be lost.

It will be well for us to look into the real value of military training for schoolboys before we adopt in a wholesale fashion obsolete militarism. The value of wooden-gunism is questionable. Physical training, vocational training, athletics, Boy Scout work, team play, and discipline are far more valuable. Military drill given in addition to these activities may be advisable. However, on this point there is still a difference of opinion. But to give formal military instruction without considering its adaptability to the methods used in modern warfare and the training incident to effective preparation for them is neither military preparedness on the one hand nor sensible educational procedure on the other.

School boards ought to organize at once vocational courses to secure state and national aid, and seek from the legislature state aid for directors of community gardens, as, from now on, these will be a permanent feature of community life. Some sort of provision ought to be made relative to bringing agriculture into the city school or taking the city boy to agriculture. A country branch of a city school is possible. Play and recreation centers must be developed. The increase of juvenile offenses in both England and France during this war has been tremendous. Many of these offenses are committed by children who are still at school. There is much evidence that owing to the absence on military service of their fathers,— and, perhaps even more, of their elder brothers,— the industrial employment of their mothers, the darkened streets, and other circumstances, many school children are suffering from the lack of proper care and discipline and are exposed to serious risks of deterioration. These conditions have been mitigated through the establishment of evening play centers, which provide the children with suitable occupation and amusement after school hours.

The principal of a school can play a large part in a war-emergency program. He can develop the idea of War Savings among the children in his school. Announcement has been made that the government intends to develop the War Savings Certificate plan of England. These certificates are perhaps better adapted to persons of small means than a Liberty Bond. The United States Treasury Department has set forth a plan for advertising and selling these certificates through the public schools of the nation. The aim is to have every pupil an owner of a "little baby bond" and a participant in a democratic plan of government security. A campaign for thrift has been started. The schools must do their part.

The principal can organize patriotic meetings at which he can explain the purposes of the Red Cross, the Liberty Loan, and the garden and conservation movements. He can distribute pamphlets relating to war service. In a small community he can be the leader of the Red Cross movement, only he must always remember that he is to work with state and national organizations and is not to write to Washington when he can perhaps step across the street to local headquarters or write directly to state headquarters. Of course, he will follow closely the printed directions with reference to bandages, shipping, etc., for the general organization has put more thought into it and gained more experience than he could possibly gather.

Obviously the principal ought to allow no competition between school organizations and local organizations. If the local organization is strong and effective, he ought to work under it. If it is not, he may well work over it. By all means he should inform pupils of the meaning of the war, that they in turn may carry word to their parents; and such work is not always limited to districts where people are foreign born. There may be as much need for such work in the West as in New York City. A Western farmer is reported as saying that he did not care who owned the country or whether the Germans took it or not so long as he sold his wheat crop.

The principal may direct a state census on some particular data for which state authorities may call. He should bring together various bulletins issued by state and national governments which concern food production and conservation, sanitation, public health, nursing, dietetics, etc., and by publishing lists of such material in newspapers and posting them on school bulletin boards, bring the information within them to the people who need it most. He should make the hall exercises in the school mean more than ever. Let us hope that " America " may be sung with more vim, and that the principal will know the second stanza. The " Marseillaise " and other national songs of our allies may be sung. Of course a service flag made by the girls in the school hangs prominently in the assembly hall, and each of its stars speaks for a teacher, a student, or a graduate who represents the life-giving contribution of the school to the cause of democracy.

The country-school principal has a great deal to do. His work differs from that of the city principal in that he may be a recognized leader in almost everything, while the city principal must necessarily coöperate with individuals and organizations. The principal in the open country can be the local agent for seed and fertilizer and for the distribution of farmers' bulletins. In fact, he may be the local representative for the state departments of education, of agriculture, of labor, and of health.

He ought to use judgment in excusing boys from school for farm work. He will know the exact circumstances under which a boy goes to work. He will know whether he is working on his father's farm or that of a neighbor. He can help that boy with his lessons so that he can do some studying at home and keep up with his classes. And in the late fall, when the boys return to school from their farm work, he can organize a special class in order that they may satisfactorily make up their studies. This extra work on his part and that of his coworkers will make one of the answers to the call to the colors which comes to every man and woman in this country.

A city principal can organize an agricultural course in his city school, and obtain a state-aided teacher for giving agricultural theory in the winter in connection with biological science, and have this teacher take a group of boys into the country in the spring. He can always think of his boys as going out to farm work on the basis of an organized group, and on that basis only. A teacher from his school might go with these boys and serve as their leader. It is probable that educational experiments of this nature will lead eventually to country branches of city schools.

It is clear that the industrial and trade schools, because of the very nature of their purpose, may render unusual service, but they must start out with the idea that they are to take their directions from the state boards of control of vocational education rather than go off at a tangent independent of any state or national movement. It must be remembered that provision has been made for a national system of vocational education with a Federal Board of Vocational Education guiding it, and that every state board having charge of vocational education is working in conjunction with the national board. We must keep in mind that the Federal Board of Vocational Education is in close touch with the National Council of Defense at Washington, and consequently with all departments of the national government which concern war measures. For a local school to jeopardize its chances for national and state aid through failure to follow a program provided by these authorities, or to develop types of work which are out of accord with national needs, will not be the part of wisdom or common sense. These schools must not forget that their primary function is to make mechanics and not army supplies, but if they are called upon to do the latter work, or if they can do it effectively, they must make it educational in its aim and not merely productive work.

State officials ought to have inventories made of the equipment of the vocational schools, with a census of the experience and training of the instructors, and a state study ought to be made of plans to train workers for the different branches needed. Such a study would point out how the semiskilled may become skilled, how the unskilled may become semiskilled, how the necessary training may be given to specialist tool makers, and how there can be developed a type of industrial work suitable for women and girls.

The directors of trade schools will provide opportunities for the training of foremen in evening classes, or at other times if necessary, using methods of instruction which will increase their skill in dealing with green help or unskilled laborers. These men will adjust the evening schools to run the year round, and also provide for off-time classes.

In vocational schools of the commercial order, of which we have very few in the country, provision will be made for short-unit courses in commercial practice for women and girls to fit them to take the place of men drafted.

As has already been stated, it is very likely that the day vocational schools will have comparatively few pupils during the war period, as young persons who ordinarily go to these schools will have readily obtained work in factories. However, such youth can still be instructed if the school will go to the factory and there establish training courses.

The present is a good time to develop commercial courses which have a vocational purpose, and which have methods more in accord with the definition of vocational training. The commercial departments in the majority of our high schools rather indifferently train stenographers, typists, and clerks. They do not even attempt to train salesmen and saleswomen, index and statistical clerks, comptometer operators, etc. Very few of the commercial courses have either the definiteness of aim of the industrial and trade schools or the practical contact with actual commercial practice which will be necessary if they are to meet the requirements of modern business. Commercial schools have not yet caught the spirit of part-time, off-time, or short-unit programs.

The manual-training teacher will find plenty to do; that is, if the state departments of education furnish him definite data and specifications for war-emergency work. It will be practically useless for him to carry on special work in any large way unless the field of service of the boy workers is organized in some such way as is the Red Cross work. If boxes are needed for packing supplies, a working drawing of the same ought to be furnished by the state department. If hospital furniture, such as bed racks and tables, is needed, the articles should be standardized in order that they may be made in quantities and may be serviceable when they reach the source of need. The same is true of splints. The reason for the great accomplishment of the French and Canadian boys in the making of splints used temporarily on the field of service is that they have been furnished with very definite directions as to size, material, and method of making.

It cannot be too emphatically stated that the war-service work of the elementary and secondary schools needs definite direction from the state departments of education if the unity of effort based upon directions common to all are to result not only in effective work but also in fulfilling the social and civic purposes which are behind the service.

This is an opportune time for the manual-training teacher to abandon his set of models. They should have been set aside long ago. His war-service duties will give an additional motive for socializing his work. In small cities and villages where there is plenty of land available for cultivation the director of manual training, on the first of May, ought to change his title and assume his duties as director of community gardens. He should have been preparing for this work by giving instruction in garden work in the manual-training room during March and April. Meanwhile he should have interested adults of the community in the plan of a garden where both old and young might work, and should have brought together civic forces to accomplish the purpose — a purpose which is educational, social, recreational, and useful.

Dealing with boys under fifteen, as the average manual-training teacher will, it is possible for him to develop a type of manual arts which will serve to create or arouse a set of industrial interests helpful to the boy in determining his life career. With every temptation to a pupil to leave school, the manual-training teacher will now have an unusual opportunity to make his work so attractive and economically so helpful that the boy may see the advantage of paying no attention to industrial-service inducements.

This is a time for increasing the field of usefulness of the industrial arts in connection with the problems involved in the junior high school. This type of school is certain to meet with increased favor during and after the war, and the reasons are both educational and administrative.

So much has already been said in several places in this book about the service which cooking and sewing teachers may render, that it is hardly necessary in this place to do more than give a very brief summary. As supplies for cooking lessons become more expensive, the cooking teacher must make more of demonstrations to pupils, and less, perhaps, of actual practice. The war recipes which she uses must be mimeographed or printed and given the pupils to take home. She must organize classes for adults in unit courses and hold them afternoons and evenings. In fact, she might well have the mothers come with the children during the regular session and receive some special instructions which the children receive. She will be busy the year round; her larger work will begin when the schools close, in that she will start her canning and community-club work. A situation can easily be conceived wherein she will have in reality very little teaching responsibility in the classroom. She will be looked upon as the community organizer for all types of food conservation, and some of her older girls will, in all probability, be teaching in the regular classes. Of course, she will interest all the children in the school in saving bottles, jars, crocks, large-mouthed bottles, tumblers, small wooden pails, etc. for containers for the jams, preserves, and fruit juices which will be put up. She will obtain all the new bulletins on processes of drying and dehydrating. Perhaps she may have initiative enough to discover a fruit crop which will not be picked except through her efforts. Perhaps she will find an orphan asylum in the community filled with boys and girls who can pick this fruit crop.

The sewing teacher has more than enough to do. If the Red Cross chapter does not keep her busy, then she can keep the chapter active. With the price of materials as high as it is now and the quality as poor, there is plenty of opportunity

to look over, in every home, the last year's ward-
robe. She might organize a Thrift Club. Enthusiastic youth will do almost anything under the
name of "club."

It is to be hoped that every girl in the school
above the age of ten will enroll in the sewing
class and not sit idly by while a few do all the
work. Very likely the household-arts teacher will
organize a home-cadet unit, just as the boys
will be organized into farm-cadet units. The
girls will have their pledge of loyalty and perhaps will wear their chevrons, badges, or buttons,
and will enroll for specific work in food, clothing,
or shelter projects.

The agricultural teacher will have more than he
can do. An effective teacher in normal periods is
always busy with his supervision of home-project
work, preparation of material for classroom teaching, gathering of laboratory exhibits, etc. But in
war time he must carry on his shoulders still larger
burdens. In the early spring he will discontinue
his formal agricultural teaching to the special vocational group and broaden his work to include those
who have not regularly enrolled in the agricultural
course. To the latter he will give some very definite
suggestions for immediate use on the farm; while
the boys who have been with him all winter will

be excused from school to give their entire time to their home projects. To those who have recently come into the class there will be given special work in the classroom which they may practice outside of school hours and which they can follow for full time during the summer.

He will have a good deal to do with the farm-cadet idea, and in the winter he will doubtless be thinking of the type of camp which he will establish or with which he will be connected. He may decide that he can do best by organizing a labor-distributing camp on his own initiative, or that he will serve as an assistant at the state-farm training camp, or that he will take his boys, if they are village boys, to the outskirts of the village and establish a coöperative camp; or he may get in touch with the teacher of biology in a city school and offer the country schoolhouse and his services for a training camp made up of city boys. It is assumed that he is in close touch with the county farm agent; perhaps he is the local representative of the club work which the United States Department of Agriculture is promoting; and, of course, he is taking the responsibility of acting as agent in his territory for the United States Boys' Working Reserve, — a really wonderful organization full of immense possibilities.

This Boys' Working Reserve movement started under the auspices of the United States Department of Labor in coöperation with the Council of National Defense, for the purpose of mobilizing young men between the ages of 16 and 21 for productive labor in the war emergency.

During the summer of 1917 the Reserve confined its activities principally to giving federal recognition to those youths who, as members of state organizations, had worked at least three weeks on farms or in food production. At present it is organized in 40 states and in the District of Columbia. Recently it has extended its activities to include industrial occupations. Each boy who is physically fit and who, with the consent of his parents, has taken the oath of service, is enrolled as a recruit and given an enrollment button and a certificate bearing the great seal of the United States. When he has worked faithfully and capably for the stated period, he is awarded a federal bronze badge of honor.

After January 1, 1918, thirty-six days of eight hours each are to be required on the farm or in food production in order to earn the badge. In industrial occupations the boy will be required to work at least sixty days of eight hours in some occupation considered essential in helping the nation in the conduct of the war, in order to receive recognition.

The national director, Mr. William E. Hall, encourages every boy to remain in school and in spare time to pursue some vocational training to make himself capable of performing a productive war service, in the expectation that he will be awarded a badge of honor when he has actually entered an essential occupation. It is expected that we shall soon see a registered army of young men ordinarily not available, which may be used to fill the gaps in the labor ranks caused by war activities.

The Reserve has been indorsed by President Wilson in the following language:

Permit me to express my great appreciation of the work undertaken by the United States Boys' Working Reserve of the Employment Service of Department of Labor. To give to the young men between the ages of 16 and 21 the privilege of spending their spare time in productive enterprise without interrupting their studies at school, while their older brothers are battling in the trenches and on the seas, must greatly increase the means of providing for the forces at the front and the maintenance of those whose services are needed here. It is a high privilege, no less than a patriotic duty, to help support the nation by devoted and intelligent work in this great crisis.

Theodore Roosevelt, in writing of the good work which the Reserve is doing, says, in part:

I am glad that you intend to encourage the training of the boys to prepare for some essential industry where they can take the place of a man called to the front. One of the great benefits you confer is that of making the boy realize that he is part of Uncle Sam's team; that he is doing his share in this great war; that he holds his services in trust for the nation; and that though it is proper to consider the question of material gain and the question of his own desires, yet that what he must most strongly consider at this time is where his services will do most good to our people as a whole.

The teachers of America, as well as the boys, are making themselves a part of Uncle Sam's team; and they too hold their services in trust for the nation. The Junior Red Cross movement in the schools has swept the country. The school children have advertised and sold bonds of the second Liberty Loan.[1] The teachers of cooking are serving as local representatives for the food administrator at Washington. Agricultural teachers have pledged themselves as community workers for the summer of 1918. Manual-training teachers are developing plans for substituting garden projects in the spring for the manual-training models of the schoolroom. Technical colleges and institutes are filled with students in uniform. Industrial and trade schools on the seacoast are planning to discard their house

[1] In New York City 63,900 applications for bonds, having a total value of $7,881,100, were obtained directly by principals, teachers, and pupils, and forwarded by the principals to the local Bond committee or the banks.

carpentry for shipbuilding courses. County superintendents of schools are studying government bulletins for the last word in preserving and drying
farm products on a large scale, in order that they
may give directions to the schools. Teachers in
academic schools have enlisted for service on relief,
loan, garden, thrift, and conservation committees.
Men who were leaders and supervisors of farm-
cadet camps in 1917 are planning for similar work
in the future on a larger and improved basis. Programs for teachers' institutes and state associations
of teachers now include the topics: "What can our
schools do in war time?" and "Our schools after
the war."

These efforts of the teachers and the pupils respond to our President's appeal that each of us
must do his share in making the world safe for
democracy.

At present, to be sure, we center our thoughts
on how to make the world safe for democracy. But
what of the future? What of the contribution of
the schools after the war? Should not the schools
then center their aims and methods on making
democracy safe for the world? If the people themselves are to be masters, must they not be provided
with an education making for mastership? Is it
not well for us to examine our present schools to

determine whether they are making a democracy which will be safe for the world? Have we a system of education which actually gives an opportunity for every child to make the most of himself? Have we a liberalized course of study which actually stimulates and develops intellectual and æsthetic interests in music, art, literature, science, travel, and history? Have we evolved a socialized education developing moral habits, civic incentives, possession and use of ethical ideals and standards for a successful group life? Has our formative process been able to bring about refinements of social behavior beyond the point required for group participation? Have we arrived at the point where we can say that our people have even the common culture which it is expected all members of a democracy shall possess, to say nothing about the development of individual culture, which is a possession of the interested individual and his congenial fellows? How far have we gone in recognizing that "by-education" which comes through a child's self-direction of his natural or spontaneous learning instincts and impulses?

How much have we accomplished in giving educational and vocational guidance to children between the ages of 12 and 16? What has been done in the way of fulfilling the national obligation to teach the strangers within our gates our language and the principles and forms of our civic life? What has been our program for subnormals in order that they may be prepared for independent living in the competitive social order? Have we established clear-cut distinctions between subnormal and crippled cases that must remain custodial and those that can be prepared for independent existence? What are we doing in the way of education for delinquents? To what extent have we utilized the discovery that these antisocial manifestations of youth are results of heredity, or of inferior homes, or of a lack of playgrounds, or of poor schools?

Have the schools missed a great opportunity for giving moral, civic, and physical training to youth by failing to absorb the Boy Scout and Camp Fire Girl movements and thus failing to grasp the full educational significance of the methods adopted by those who so well understand adolescent youth? Are the disciplinary methods of the teachers and the general internal management of the schools such as will develop among pupils a democracy which is safe even in the schoolroom? What have we done in determining what is desirable and feasible for extending general education to average adults who have early entered upon specialized occupations?

How far have we gone in our program of vocational education to recognize and to provide for the influence of automatic machinery upon the physical, mental, and vocational welfare of workers? Have we so thoroughly grasped the idea of an educational democracy that no child in our schools is disadvantaged by the section of the state or of the country in which he happens to be born?

Have we in our vocational training set up any program for the industrial training of women which recognizes that the modern problem of women's work concerns the following of some productive vocation away from home? Have we even begun to realize that every person should have definite vocational training with such distinctive purpose back of it that it will produce the skill, knowledge, ideals, and general experience that function in distinct callings?

Have we even thought of a program of education for leisure which will develop enduring tastes and interests established toward the enrichment of the individual and indirectly of social life? Do we fully understand that to make democracy safe for the world all people should have some leisure or time apart from vocational, civic, and physical necessities of life, that such leisure should be filled with sociability, amusement, recreation, and satisfaction of the æsthetic and physical desires, and that the public schools must in some measure provide for these?

Will a democracy proclaiming equality of opportunity as its ideal require an education which unites from the beginning of the child's school life, and for all pupils of the school, learning and social application, ideas and practice, work and recognition of the meaning of what is done? Or can a democracy be developed by dividing the public-school system into parts, one of which pursues traditional methods with incidental improvements, and another in which children "learn through their hands" and are given only the "essential features" of the traditional bookwork?

All that the schools are now doing in war time, and much more which they are not yet doing, to make the world safe for democracy, may be effectively used after war time to make democracy safe for the world.

INDEX

ANNOUNCEMENTS

BOOKS OF WAR-TIME INTEREST

UPON the schools falls in great measure the responsibility of training and fitting the nation for service. To support the schools in fulfilling this tremendous duty is the purpose of the two following books.

OUR SCHOOLS IN WAR TIME—AND AFTER

By ARTHUR D. DEAN, Professor of Vocational Education, Teachers College, Columbia University, and Supervising Officer, Bureau of Vocational Training, New York State Military Training Commission. 335 pages, $1.25.

A BOOK to challenge the spirit of every loyal American. It describes the war work being done by schools in this country and others, and gives practical suggestions for promoting the work in this country. Conservation of food and other lessons in thrift, vocational education, Red Cross and other community work, and reëducation of the disabled are only a few of the important topics emphasized.

Eight inserts of photographic illustrations concretely visualize the subject for the reader.

FOOD PROBLEMS

By A. N. FARMER, Superintendent of Schools, Evanston, Ill., and JANET R. HUNTINGTON, State Department of Public Instruction, Wis. 27 cents, list price, or 20 cents, net, to boards of education, teachers, and schools ; carriage extra.

THIS book aims to introduce lessons of thrift into the home by utilizing the enormous influence of the schools upon national thought and habit. It embodies in arithmetical problems of the most practical nature principles upheld by the Food Administration. Where the book has been studied it has been found to fulfill a two-fold purpose : pupils have worked with greater energy and good will, and both the children and their parents have attacked with more determination the most important, the underlying, problem — food conservation. To insure for this book the immediate and wide distribution that it merits, Ginn and Company are offering it at an unusually low price.

GINN AND COMPANY PUBLISHERS

INDUSTRIAL ARTS IN
THE SCHOOL

EXAMPLES OF INDUSTRIAL EDUCATION

By FRANK MITCHELL LEAVITT, The University of Chicago. 330 pages, $1.25

THE movement for industrial education is a part of a recent great educational advance. This volume discusses the history and practice of the movement to bring about universal and appropriate education, especially in its relation to existing social, economic, and educational institutions. The author outlines a constructive plan for organization of this type of education by public schools and gives many helpful suggestions for bringing such organization into vital relation with the present system. Full descriptions of existing classes and schools serve as examples to illustrate the general principles of their classification.

FINE AND INDUSTRIAL ARTS IN ELEMENTARY
SCHOOLS

By WALTER SARGENT, The University of Chicago. 132 pages, illustrated, 75 cents

THE present wide acceptance of the manual arts as an important part of general education is rapidly removing them from the class of special subjects. The purpose of this book is to present some considerations upon questions arising from this readjustment. The distinctive functions of the various subjects taught under the head of manual arts, the organization of progressive instruction, and reasonable standards of attainment from year to year are among the subjects given careful consideration. The book includes a survey of the progression of work in the elementary grades, which forms the basis for the more detailed suggestions which follow.

HOW CHILDREN LEARN TO DRAW

By WALTER SARGENT and ELIZABETH E. MILLER, The University of Chicago. 264 pages, illustrated, $1.00

A NEW and decidedly fresh viewpoint is at once apparent in this book, which treats drawing as a means of self-expression, as entirely natural as talking or writing. The book combines, in subject matter, theory as to what is to be accomplished, practical reports as to how these aims have been accomplished, particularly in the Elementary School of the School of Education (The University of Chicago), and definite suggestions for improvement of methods. It will be found an excellent volume for reading circles as well as for use in normal-training classes and departments of education.

GINN AND COMPANY PUBLISHERS

BOOKS FOR TEACHERS

Allen: Civics and Health . . . .
Bloomfield: Readings in Vocational Guidance . . . .
Brigham: Geographic Influences in American History . . .
Curtis: Play and Recreation for the Open Country . . . . .
Davis: Vocational and Moral Guidance . . . .
Finlay-Johnson: The Dramatic Method of Teaching . . . .
Gesell: The Normal Child and Primary Education . . . . .
Hall: Aspects of Child Life and Education . . . .
Hodge: Nature Study and Life . . . .
Johnson: Education by Plays and Games . . . .
Johnson: What to do at Recess . . . .
Jones: Education as Growth . . . .
Judd: Psychology of High-School Subjects . . . .
Kastman and Köhler: Swedish Song Games . . . .
Kern: Among Country Schools . . . .
Leavitt: Examples of Industrial Education . . . .
Leiper: Language Work in Elementary Schools . . . . . .
Lincoln: Everyday Pedagogy. . . . .
Moore: What is Education? . . . .
Moral Training in the Public Schools . . . .
Palmer: Play Life in the First Eight Years . . . .
Parker: History of Modern Elementary Education . . . . .
Parker: Methods of Teaching in High Schools . . . . . .
Phillips: An Elementary Psychology . . . .
Prince: Courses of Studies and Methods of Teaching . . . .
Read: An Introductory Psychology . . . .
Sargent: Fine and Industrial Arts in Elementary Schools . .
Sargent and Miller: How Children Learn to Draw . . . . .
Scott: Social Education . . . .
Smith: The Teaching of Arithmetic . . . .
Tompkins: Philosophy of School Management . . . . . .
Tompkins: Philosophy of Teaching . . . .
Williams: Gardens and their Meaning . . . .
Wiltse: Place of the Story in Early Education, and Other Essays

GINN AND COMPANY Publishers

BOOKS ON
VOCATIONAL GUIDANCE

BUSINESS EMPLOYMENTS

By FREDERICK J. ALLEN, Vocation Bureau of Boston. 218 pages, $1.00.

A COMPREHENSIVE and thorough-going survey of business in its three typical divisions — manufacture, trade, finance. This study has been prepared from direct examination of the most modern and up-to-date material available on the business organization and business methods of to-day. In its absolute reliability and accuracy it will serve excellently well the young person who wishes to learn of the nature, extent, and opportunities of the business world.

READINGS IN VOCATIONAL GUIDANCE

By MEYER BLOOMFIELD, Director of the Vocation Bureau of Boston. xv + 723 pages, $2.25.

THIS volume represents an extensive collection of the most noteworthy literature on vocational guidance. It is not merely a careful compilation, but is as well a carefully organized presentation, richly suggestive for all who are interested in the subject. Much material here included is not elsewhere available.

VOCATIONAL AND MORAL GUIDANCE

By JESSE BUTTRICK DAVIS, Vocational Director of Schools, Grand Rapids, Mich. 303 pages, $1.25.

A SIGNIFICANT volume into the preparation of which have gone several years of practical experiment upon the problems of vocational guidance. The result is a book invaluable in its wealth of definite and workable suggestions for the organization and administration of vocational work in schools.

OCCUPATIONS

By ENOCH BURTON GOWIN, New York University, and WILLIAM ALONZO WHEATLEY, Superintendent of Schools, Middletown, Conn. 357 pages, illustrated, $1.20.

THIS is a textbook for the student's own use, planned to cover both vocational guidance and vocational information, with the emphasis strongly upon the latter. Part I sets forth the importance of vocational preparation; Part II is a survey of various occupations; and Part III shows the student how to apply the knowledge gained in Parts I and II. Besides being intrinsically interesting the book is well organized for class use.

GINN AND COMPANY PUBLISHERS